Virtues & Values

Laura Blanco – Silvia Carbonell

Illustrated by Rosa Maria Curto

Bonneville Books
Springville, Utah

SAYVILLE LIBRARY

Contents

1 WISDOM

• *Proverbs 8:10*
Receive my instruction, and not silver; and knowledge rather than choice gold.

People young and old—even small children—want to know how to make the right choices in life.

• **CHILDREN SOMETIMES SAY**
- When I grow up, I want to make a lot of money.

• **WHAT DO WE ANSWER?**
- We need money to live, but it is much more important to be happy.

• **A FEW MINUTES TO THINK**
Life is full of choices.
The virtue of wisdom helps us to make the right choices and do the right things.

Let's listen to a story about a wise King

THE STORY

First book of 1 Kings 3:16–28

One day two women went to see King Solomon. One of them said: "I gave birth to a child while this woman was in my house and three days later she also had a child. One night, this woman's child died and, in the middle of the night, she got up, took my child and laid her dead son beside me. I woke up in the middle of the night to feed my child and saw the child was dead, but I realized it was not my own."

The other woman shouted: "That's a lie! The dead child was yours; the live child is mine!"
The king ordered: "Bring me a sword." When they brought it, he said: "Cut the child in half and give a half to each of the women."

The mother of the live child begged the king: "Please don't kill the child, my lord! Keep the child alive and give him to her!"
The other woman, on the contrary, said: "The child cannot be for you or for me. Let them cut the child up!"
Then the king gave his verdict: "Do not kill the child; give him to the first woman. She is the mother."
The people of Israel heard about the king's sentence, and they thanked God for giving them a king who was wise and good.

What do you think?
REFLECTION

- Do you think the King would have allowed the child to be cut in half?
- Why did the child's real mother want to give her child to the other woman?
- If you had been the child's mother, what would you have done?
- King Solomon showed he was wise. How would you describe wisdom?

This week . . .
I will do my best to make right choices and help others do the same.

2 **Joy**

• *Psalm 122:1*
I was glad when they said unto me, Let us go into the house of the Lord.

It is good to go to church; it is a place where we meet people, share our faith, and think about what is happening in our lives.

• **CHILDREN SOMETIMES SAY**
- I get bored in church because I have to keep quiet and it all takes too long.

• **WHAT DO WE ANSWER?**
- We go to church to praise God and to listen to Jesus's word. We ought to be quiet.

• **A FEW MINUTES TO THINK**
This is a common complaint from our children; but, if you get them to participate in the service—getting them to read or sing, helping them give thanks, and helping them understand what is happening—then they are happier about going to church.

LISTEN
Being quiet helps us learn how to listen and how to take time to think.

A listening game

GAME

1. Find three people to play this game.
2. One person is a speaker, one is a listener, and one is an observer.
3. The speaker tells a story for two minutes, and the listener listens.
4. The listener cannot speak; but can only say "mmm" or "oh" or "ahh."
5. The observer makes sure that the speaker and the listener do what they are supposed to and keeps track of the time.
6. This is repeated three times so that each child gets to be a speaker, a listener and an observer. At the end, the children should talk about what it was like to play each of these parts.

This week . . .
I will notice the joy I experience when I listen to someone or when someone listens to me.

It is not as hard as you think!

REFLECTION

- Just before lunch or supper if at home, or during a break at school, get everyone in the group to be absolutely quiet for a couple of minutes, thinking about something each one wants.
- When time is up, each person, child or adult, gets the chance to tell the others what he or she was thinking about; and everyone should listen.

We all need to listen to others, and we all want to be listened to.

3 FrienDshiP

• *John 15:15*
Henceforth I call you not servants; for the servant knoweth not what his lord doeth: but I have called you friends; for all things that I have heard of my Father I have made known unto you.

God wants to be your friend, give you good advice, and be close to you when you need him.

• **CHILDREN SOMETIMES SAY**
- When we were playing football in the park, we had an argument because one of the boys said he scored a goal; but he was off side. He said it was valid. I am not his friend anymore. He cheats!

• **WHAT DO WE ANSWER?**
- You should have helped that boy realize what he had done and still be a good friend to him.

• **A FEW MINUTES TO THINK**
When something like this happens, the natural reaction for children is to say they don't want to be friends anymore. It is important to help them think about the value of friendship.

My frieNDs

LET'S CHAT

- Do you have friends?
- Why are they your friends?
- What do you know about them?
- What do they do for you, and what do you do for them?
- Talk about the importance of looking after your friends.

This week . . .
I will thank God for the gift of friendship, and I will be a good friend to . . .

The gift of frieNDship

GAME

Material

Some cards with some unfinished sentences on them, like

- I like being with my friends and . . .
- I tried to be a good friend to someone when I . . .
- I listened to my friend when . . .
- I like it when my friend shares . . .

Get everyone to sit in a circle. The pack of cards is passed from one child to the next. Each child will finish the sentence on the top card of the pack and place it at the bottom of the pack. Those who cannot think of anything to finish the sentence are "out," and the game continues until there is only one child left. That child is the winner.

4 Simplicity

• *Acts 2:46*
And they, continuing daily with one accord in the temple, and breaking bread from house to house, did eat their meat with gladness and singleness of heart.

The first Christians lived in a community. They went to the temple every day. They shared what they had without making a big fuss.

• **CHILDREN SOMETIMES SAY**
- If I wear lots of bracelets and necklaces, I will look more elegant, won't I?

• **WHAT DO WE ANSWER?**
- You will not look more elegant because you wear more things; often, simply wearing one thing will make you more elegant.

• **A FEW MINUTES TO THINK**
Share the following reflection with the children:
If you are walking along a street and look at the window in a shoe shop, you will probably find it hard to notice all the shoes on display. However, if the window displays just one pair of shoes, or three pairs at the most, you will surely notice them because of the simple and elegant way they are displayed.

What's the Difference?

AN OUTING

If you live in a town where there are gothic or baroque churches, take an opportunity to go out and visit them. If not, look at pictures of these churches on the internet or in books.

Look for ornamental elements:
- How many figures of animals can you see?
- Can you see any heavenly figures?
- Where is Jesus?
- What are they doing?
- Are there any floral elements? Do you know what they are called?

Imagine the amount of hard work it took to make these churches.

On another day, you might visit a Roman church if there is one nearby (or, again, you can look at pictures of them on the internet or in a book).
- Notice the simple design of these churches.
- Does the church you saw the other day look like this one?
- What differences do you notice?

The children will notice the lack of details—the simplicity in structure and in the paintings. If not, stress the point, showing them that simplicity is pleasant. The same applies to a monument, a picture, or a fashion show on TV.

Let's cut out Paper Clothes

HANDICRAFT

Material
Outlines (page 108), tracing paper, plain paper, crayons or markers, pencil, scissors.
1. Print out the images or place the tracing paper over the outline for both the boy and the girl (page 108) with their clothes (pages 110–13) and let the children color them.
2. Children can draw more clothes by placing the tracing paper over the outlines and drawing the clothes they want.
3. To make the clothes of a thicker kind of paper, cut the drawing out and use it as a pattern.
4. Color the clothes and cut them out.
5. Children can play with the outline drawings—dress them, change their clothes, and play with them.

This week . . .
I will notice the things around me that are attractive because they are simple.

5 Self-Discipline

- *Proverbs 4:13*
Take fast hold of instruction; let her not go: keep her; for she is thy life.

We all have to learn new things; we never stop learning!

- ● **CHILDREN SOMETIMES SAY**
- - I don't feel like doing homework. I'll do it tomorrow.

- ● **WHAT DO WE ANSWER?**
- - If you leave it until tomorrow, you will have tomorrow's and today's—double homework. You won't have time to play. It is much better to do some homework every day and then play every day. Otherwise, you will have to work all day with no time off for fun.
- - It's the same thing with sweets. If you keep some for each day, you will enjoy them every day; but if you eat them up in just one day, you are likely to end up with a tummy ache.

- ● **A FEW MINUTES TO THINK**
Self-discipline is hard! It takes effort, but it is rewarding. For example, if you want to play a musical instrument, you must practice every day—and, in the end, you will be able to play beautiful music!

Chocolate truffles

COOKING
With the help of an adult

Ingredients

7 oz. of baking chocolate
1 small carton of cream
1 dessert spoon of superfine sugar
½ tsp. vanilla extract

1. Help the children melt the chocolate. Stir it until it melts.
2. In a large mixing bowl, beat the cream until it is smooth. Gradually add the sugar, stirring it until well blended. Add the melted chocolate and vanilla; mix well. Refrigerate for 1 hour or until firm.
3. Shape into small balls. Roll in chopped nuts, cocoa, or toasted coconut, if desired.
4. Store in the refrigerator.

Agree with the children when they are going to have the truffles. Share this happy moment with the family, or with friends, but eat just one truffle a day. Perhaps on the last day they can have two—as a reward for having made them.

How steady is your hand?

HANDICRAFT-EXPERIMENT
With the help of an adult

Material

Clay, wire, a wooden ball with a hole.

The stick

1. Pass a piece of wire through the ball.
2. Bend the wire a little at the end where the ball is so it will not fall off.
3. Shape the other end of the wire to make a ring (as in the picture).

The structure

1. Model two small blocks out of clay.
2. Bend a piece of wire (as in the picture).
3. Stick one end of the wire in the clay.
4. Pass the wire ring through the other end and then stick the end in the second piece of clay.

Can you move the stick along the wire without touching it? Can you do it faster?

This week . . .
I will be more self-disciplined by . . .

WEEK

6 Beauty

• *Psalm 8:3–4*

When I consider thy heavens, the work of thy fingers, the moon and the stars, which thou hast ordained;
What is man, that thou art mindful of him? and the son of man, that thou visitest him?

Think about the world around us. Notice the beauty of the trees and the flowers, of all the different people and animals. Look up at the sky and the clouds: the sun in the daytime and the moon and stars at night.

• **Children sometimes say**

- Did God really create the whole universe in just six days?

• **What do we answer?**

- The story of the creation was written a long time ago to thank and praise God for the gift of creation. In fact, many days were needed to create the world; indeed, creation is not an event fixed in the past but something that is still going on today.

• **A few minutes to think**

Read the story of the creation in the Bible (Genesis, chapter 1). Talk together about how we feel when we think about creation, for example, when it is a warm, sunny day or when it is windy or very cold; when we see a new baby or a puppy dog or kitten.
The story in the Bible tells us that on the seventh day, God rested. We too need to take time to rest after we have done our work . We go to church on Sundays to give thanks and praise to God for the gift of creation.

Fluorescent stars
HANDICRAFT

Material
Some soft plastic or cardboard, fluorescent paints, pencil, scissors or cutter, brush, glue.

Making the fluorescent stars
1. Use the templates on page 109 and draw the stars on the plastic or cardboard.
2. Cut them out and paint them.
3. When they are dry, children should ask an adult to stick them on the ceiling in their room. They will keep them company at night.

This week . . .
I will remember to thank God for . . .

Looking at the sky
OUTING—OBSERVATION

Children can ask their parents to take them outside at night to look at the moon and the stars, ideally in the countryside where there isn't as much light reflected in the sky as there is in the city.

Questions
- What does the moon look like? Is it a full moon, waning moon, new moon, half moon?
- How are the stars set in the sky?

You can use
- Maps of the stars
- Binoculars
- A telescope

Children may write down their observations in a notebook.

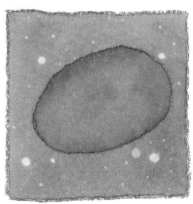

7 GooDness

• *Psalm 113:7*
He raiseth up the poor out of the dust, and lifteth the needy out of the dunghill.

The psalmist tells us about a God who is good, compassionate and just, who helps those in need no matter what their faith, race, sex, or age is.

• CHILDREN SOMETIMES SAY

- Today at school somebody tore David's jacket. David and Mark started a fight, and then a group of boys and girls joined in and all of them were against David.

• WHAT DO WE ANSWER?

- What was the point of the fight?
- How do you think David felt when everybody was against him?
- Even if David started the fight, do you think all the boys and girls should have joined in?

• A FEW MINUTES TO THINK

It is important to give children a chance to think about what happened and to talk it through with you.

Cinderella

THE STORY

In a faraway country, long, long ago there was a girl whose mother had died. The father and the child were happy living together, but he still missed his wife, so he decided to marry again.

The stepmother was not very nice to the girl and neither were her two daughters. When the father was away on a trip, the girl, whom they called Cinderella, had to do all the household chores: sewing, cooking, cleaning, and ironing.

One day, the king invited all the young girls in his kingdom to a ball with the prince, his son. Cinderella said: "How I would love to attend! But I have not finished the housework and, even if I could go, I have nothing to wear."

Then a fairy appeared and said: "Don't cry, Cinderella, you will go to the ball." And with a touch of her magic wand, she transformed Cinderella's dress into the most beautiful gown she could ever have imagined; and she changed her old shoes into silver slippers.

"But how will I get to the dance?" asked Cinderella. And then the fairy transformed a pumpkin into a carriage and some mice into horses and a coachman.

"But," said the fairy to Cinderella, "you must come back at midnight, before the clock strikes twelve."

When Cinderella went into the palace, she captivated the prince with her beauty, and he danced with her all night. Everybody wondered who that pretty girl was. But when the bells started ringing at midnight, Cinderella left in a hurry and she lost one of her silver slippers on the steps of the palace. The prince picked up the shoe, but he could not find Cinderella. The king then ordered one of his servants to find the owner of the silver slipper.

All the young ladies in the kingdom tried, even Cinderella's stepsisters, but the shoe would not fit anyone. The King's servant insisted that Cinderella should try on the slipper as well even though her stepmother didn't want her to.

When Cinderella tried on the silver slipper and they saw it fit her perfectly, her stepmother and her stepsisters were filled with envy. The servant took Cinderella to the palace, the prince married her, and they lived happily ever after.

LET'S CHAT

- Who is the unhappy person in this story?
- Do you know why the girl is called Cinderella?
- The psalm says: "he lifteth the needy out of the dunghill." What does that say about Cinderella in this story?
- Who helps her to become a princess?
- What is the attitude of Cinderella's stepsisters and stepmother?

This week . . .
I will be kind to someone by . . .

8 Love

• *Acts 9:36*

Now there was at Joppa a certain disciple named Tabitha, which by interpretation is called Dorcas: this woman was full of good works and almsdeeds which she did.

Dorcas had many friends. She made clothes for people in need, and she liked to help them. The whole town loved Dorcas because she loved her people.

● **CHILDREN SOMETIMES SAY**

- Today, during break, I helped Ann and Andrew with some math problems.

● **WHAT DO WE ANSWER?**

- That's very nice, I am proud of you.

● **A FEW MINUTES TO THINK**

Loving others means doing things and expecting nothing in return.
What kind of things can we do to be loving?
- We can visit a sick friend.
- We can help our parents.
- We can give away one of our toys to a child who has none.

Let's think about other ways we can be loving

HANDICRAFT
With the help of an adult

Let's make tea towels or napkins.

Material
Some pieces of cloth, dye, fruits or vegetables (for example, pear, potato, carrot, and apple), permanent black marker, newspaper, kitchen paper, brushes, scissors, and a knife.

1. Place a piece of cloth over some newspaper.
2. Cut the fruit or vegetable in half.
3. Dry the cut surface with some kitchen paper.
4. With a brush, apply a coat of dye to the cut surface.
5. You can use one or more colors but try not to mix them.
6. Stamp the fruit on the fabric, pressing it down firmly.

You can give a napkin or tea towel as a present to someone you love.

This week . . .
I will show my love by . . .

Food for small animals
AN OUTING

When you slice bread or make sandwiches, there are usually bread crumbs. Maybe you could collect them and put them in a bag. Then, when you go to the park or go out into your garden, you can scatter the crumbs for the birds.

When you go to the park or to a river where there are ducks or fish, you can take some dry bread with you. It is fun to break the bread into small pieces to feed the ducks and fish. These are ways you can be loving to small animals.

9 mercy

• *Jonah 4:2*

And he prayed unto the Lord, and said, I pray thee, O Lord, was not this my saying, when I was yet in my country? Therefore I fled before unto Tarshish: for I knew that thou art a gracious God, and merciful, slow to anger, and of great kindness, and repentest thee of the evil.

Jonah, after spending three days in the belly of a whale, asked God to save him, and he did. He wanted God to show him mercy as well.

• **CHILDREN SOMETIMES SAY**

- Why are we sometimes told that our teeth will fall out or our noses will grow long if we tell lies?

• **WHAT DO WE ANSWER?**

- It is just a way to tell children not to tell lies. Do you remember what happened to Pinocchio every time he told a lie?

• **A FEW MINUTES TO THINK**

Sometimes people tell lies because they are afraid. The lie may not be serious, but it breaks the bond of trust between people. It is good to talk about it so that the bond of trust can be built up again.

The story of Jonah

The Lord said to Jonah: "Go to the big city of Nineveh and tell them I am not pleased with the way they are behaving. Tell the people that in forty days Nineveh will be destroyed." But Jonah thought: "God is loving. He forgives people and lets them have a second chance. He won't destroy them. And I will look silly if I go there with God's message." So, Jonah did not do as he was told. He decided to go away on a boat instead.

Then God sent a very strong wind over the sea, and there came such a big storm that it seemed the boat would split in two. The people on the boat were very frightened. They told everyone on the boat to pray for their lives. The sea got rougher and rougher.

Jonah said he could not pray to God for help because he was running away from God.

He said: "God sent the storm." And they asked Jonah: "What do we have to do for the sea to become calm again?" He answered: "Throw me to the sea, and it will calm down." They took hold of Jonah and threw him into the water, and the sea became calm. Jonah thought he would drown, and he called out to God for help. God sent a great whale, and the whale swallowed Jonah.

For three days and three nights, Jonah was inside the belly of the whale. While he was there, Jonah begged the Lord not to let him die. God heard him and ordered the whale to spit Jonah out onto the beach.

After that, Jonah went to Nineveh and did what God had told him to do.

(You could also read or watch the story of *Pinocchio*.)

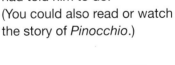

This week . . .
I will try to do my best to tell the truth and to do as I am asked to do.

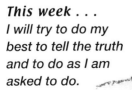

Answer and Draw

REFLECTION

- What do the stories of Jonah and Pinocchio have in common?
- A whale swallowed Jonah. What happened to Pinocchio?
- Both Jonah and Pinocchio are forgiven— even though they had not behaved in the right way. Do you know why?
- Draw the main characters in each story.

10 consistency

• *Matthew 7:12*
Therefore all things whatsoever ye would that men should do to you, do ye even so to them: for this is the law and the prophets.

Jesus tells us: love others as you love yourself. It is a fundamental principle of our behavior.

• CHILDREN SOMETIMES SAY
- Do I have to write a thank-you card now? I don't want to!

• WHAT DO WE ANSWER?
- Maybe you don't feel like it; but the person who gave you a gift did something special for you and spent some time thinking about you. If you want to receive, you also have to give.

• A FEW MINUTES TO THINK
If we teach children to think about how their actions affect others, it will help them learn to love others as they love themselves.

A special letter

CORRESPONDENCE

Make a list of friends and/or relatives you would like to send a special letter to.

Think about each person to whom you want to send a letter or an email and make it special for that person. For example:

- If it is a romantic person, you might send her a poem.
- If it is a person who likes challenges and efforts, you might send a riddle.
- If it is a person with a good imagination, you might write a story.

- If it is a person who likes to travel, send a description of a place you visited.
- If it is a person who loves cooking, you might send a recipe.
- If it is an artistic person or someone who likes your drawings you might send a drawing or collage.

There are many more ideas you might think of!

Make a list

LET'S CHAT

Encourage children to make a list of things they like or don't like other people to do to them. The list can be something like this:

This week . . .
I will send a letter or an email to . . .

	I like it when . . .	I don't like it when . . .
Mom		
Dad		
Brothers Sisters		
Friends		

11 Genuineness

• *Luke 6:43*
For a good tree bringeth not forth corrupt fruit; neither doth a corrupt tree bring forth good fruit.

If people are genuine, you will see it in the way they behave. Equally, if people are not genuine but jealous and selfish, you will see that too in the way they behave.

• **CHILDREN SOMETIMES SAY**
- In the news they were talking about plagiarism. What is plagiarism?

• **WHAT DO WE ANSWER?**
- To plagiarize is to make an exact copy of something someone else has done and to say it is yours. For example, you copy a work of art and sell it as if it were your design.

• **A FEW MINUTES TO THINK**
Being genuine is important in many areas of life—a genuine work of art, a genuine video, a genuine person, someone you can trust.

Visiting an exhibition
AN OUTING

Before setting off:
- Think about how we should behave in a public place.
- Look for information about the work we will see at the exhibition. Who is the artist, what is the style of the painting, what period is it, and what other works are there by the same artist?

At the exhibition:
- We will look at a few pictures painted by the same artist.
- What colors does the artist use?
  - What does the artist paint?
    - Are the pictures old or modern, big or small?

Back home or at school:
- We can paint a picture, trying to imitate the artist's style. (Explain that this is not plagiarism!)

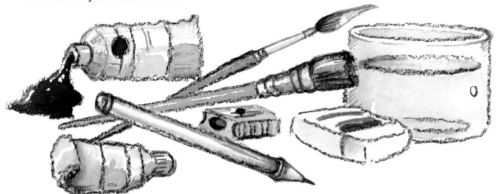

Make your own Picture
HANDICRAFT

Using whatever materials you like to draw or paint with, think of something you would like to make a picture of—not something you've copied, but something new. This will be your very own idea; it will be a genuinely original work—something unique. If it turns out well, you might even put it in a frame.

This week . . .
I will try to show that I am a genuine person by . . .

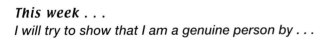

12 commitment

• *Deuteronomy 26:17*
Thou hast avouched the Lord this day to be thy God, and to walk in his ways, and to keep his statutes, and his commandments, and his judgments, and to hearken unto his voice.

Once we have decided to love the Lord and do as he tells us, you will see that he will always take care of us.

• CHILDREN SOMETIMES SAY

- My parents sometimes promise to take me to the cinema or somewhere special, but then something happens and they do not do as they promised. I get very angry because they promised but didn't keep their promise.

• WHAT DO WE ANSWER?

- Sometimes we can't keep our promises. But we should say why.

• A FEW MINUTES TO THINK

We have to learn how to make commitments.
When we promise to do something, we don't always keep our promise.
When we promise to put our toys away, for example, we don't always do it, do we?

I Promise
HANDICRAFT

Material
A sheet of paper and some markers.

Each person in the group or a member of the family should agree to do some chores. Write down what each person has agreed to do and then ask them to sign and date their task. Here is an example:

I, _____, promise to feed the goldfish and change the water in the bowl.

I, _____, promise to replenish the toilet paper in the bathroom.

I, _____, promise to pick up litter in the playground.

I, _____, promise to tidy the chairs and desks before we leave the classroom.

This week . . .
I will find something new I can do around the house, perhaps tidy my room.

Who Will Prepare Breakfast?

LET'S CHAT

We often ask children to make a commitment to do something, but we don't always show the children that adults also make commitments (such as preparing the meals, doing the laundry, the shopping, the cleaning, and so on).

It is a good idea to help the children realize that—adults and children alike—make a contribution to the household chores. They will be more willing to do their bit when they can see that everyone is helping out.

WEEK

13 Humility

• *Matthew 21:5*
Tell ye the daughter of Sion, Behold, thy King cometh unto thee, meek, and sitting upon an ass, and a colt the foal of an ass.

When Jesus entered Jerusalem, people welcomed him with palm branches.
This king is special. This king is the king of peace. This king came and lived among us. He had no special privileges.

• CHILDREN SOMETIMES SAY
- Do you have to be poor to be humble?

• WHAT DO WE ANSWER?
- No, humble people are people who aren't always drawing attention to themselves.

• A FEW MINUTES TO THINK
Sometimes, when children are young, they are impressed by important people's positions, or by material possessions. Children need to learn that even if people have important jobs or many possessions, that does not mean that they are better than others. We all rely on other people—no matter who we are.
Help the children notice the virtue of humility in the people they know, both friends and relatives; in current events; in films; or in traditional tales (see the story of Cinderella on page 17).

Jesus enters Jerusalem
DRAMATIZATION

When the people heard that Jesus was coming to Jerusalem, they collected palm branches and went out to greet him.

Many people laid their coats on the road while others cut branches from trees to make a carpet on the ground.

The crowd shouted:

- Hosanna to the son of David!
- Hosanna in the highest!
- Hosanna! Welcome to the one who comes in the name of the Lord, Hosanna!

You might like to watch this episode in movies.

This week . . .
I will think how we all need help—even the people we think are important.

A carpet made of flowers
HANDICRAFT

Material
Chalk, watering can, broom and dustpan, flowers, water.

1. Use the chalk to draw the outline of an Easter bunny, a chick, a dove, or some other object associated with Easter, on the ground outside (or on a large piece of paper if you are indoors).
2. Fill the spaces in your drawing with flowers of a specific color.
   For example:
   If you draw a dove, you will use white flowers, a chick would be yellow, an olive branch would be green. The background might be made of green leaves or yellow flowers.
3. If the carpet is to be outside, you might want to sprinkle it with water to keep it fresh for a little longer.

14 AvailaBility

• *1 Thessalonians 5:15*
See that none render evil for evil unto any man; but ever follow that which is good, both among yourselves, and to all men.

When we decide to do something for someone, we should do it happily so that the person being helped will see that we want to be there for them. It is important to be available to others—even when that sometimes means that we have to stop doing something we like doing.

● **CHILDREN SOMETIMES SAY**
- I've made my bed and set the table for breakfast. Do you want me to do anything else?

● **WHAT DO WE ANSWER?**
- No! That's wonderful. Thank you very much!

● **A FEW MINUTES TO THINK**
When children are helpful without being asked, it is important to show that we appreciate them (it will probably encourage them to be helpful more often!).

Easter eggs

HANDICRAFT
With the help of an adult

Material
Oil paint (3–4 colors), turpentine, cold water, eggs, a large and a small bowl, small jars, a stick, a piece of candle, old newspapers to cover the table, a cloth to dry your hands.

1. Fill the large bowl with cold water.
2. Put a different color of paint in each jar.
3. Add some turpentine to the paint and mix it with the stick.
4. Puncture a small hole at the two ends of each egg. Place the egg over the small bowl and blow through the hole of the small end of the egg until all of the inside is removed. Rinse the shell with cold water and let it dry thoroughly. Close the holes with melted wax.
5. Pour a small quantity of each color, separately, in the bowl with cold water without stirring it.
6. Put in the eggs and leave them there for 2 or 3 minutes. Then take the eggs out and let them dry.

This technique is called marble coloring.

This week . . .
I will be available to help by . . .

HELPING OUT
Being available means doing things for others without expecting anything in return.

Setting the Easter taBle

HANDICRAFT

At Easter, children can be asked to set the table—decorating it by putting one of the eggs they have colored at each place.

Material
The inside rolls of toilet paper, colored paper, glue, markers or paint, and scissors.

Cut the rolls into three pieces. Make each roll into an egg cup by painting it. Then put a colored label on each cup with the name of a relative or friend that you have invited to your Easter meal.
When you do something for others like this, you will see that it is better to give than to receive.

15 Trust

• *Proverbs 3:5*
Trust in the Lord with all thine heart; and lean not unto thine own understanding.

To trust is to have faith that God takes care of us and guides our lives.

• CHILDREN SOMETIMES SAY

- John said that tomorrow he would invite me to his house to play. Can I call to remind him?

• WHAT DO WE ANSWER?

- Wait! Be patient! Trust him. If he said he would call, he will call.

• A FEW MINUTES TO THINK

Learning to trust is important. A small child has absolute trust in his parents and teachers.

We should trust people, know how to wait, give others an opportunity to do what they said they would. Do you know who and what blind people trust to help them get from one place to another?

Trust game

Material

Handkerchief or piece of cloth to be used as a blindfold.

How to play

Children play in pairs. One is blindfolded and the other is not. The blindfolded one is led around a safe course (which should involve a step, turning round, and perhaps, having to go under something). The one leading has to make sure that the blindfolded one is safe. The blindfolded one has to trust the one leading him or her. Then, switch places with one another and go around the course again.

At the end, talk about what it felt like to be blindfolded and what it felt like to be responsible for the blindfolded one.

Writing a letter to friends
CORRESPONDENCE

Material

Writing paper, envelopes, stamps, pen, pencil and color pencil, friends' addresses.

Write a letter to a friend. Enclose a poem or a riddle that you received for a special occasion and you want to share. Remember to include the date and finish by saying that you trust that you will have everything back soon. Sign it. Post the letter and wait for the reply.
If you have access to a computer, you might write to your friend by email and send the document.

This week . . .
I will try to be aware of
all the people I trust . . .

TRUSTING
You can only trust someone who you know loves you and cares for you.

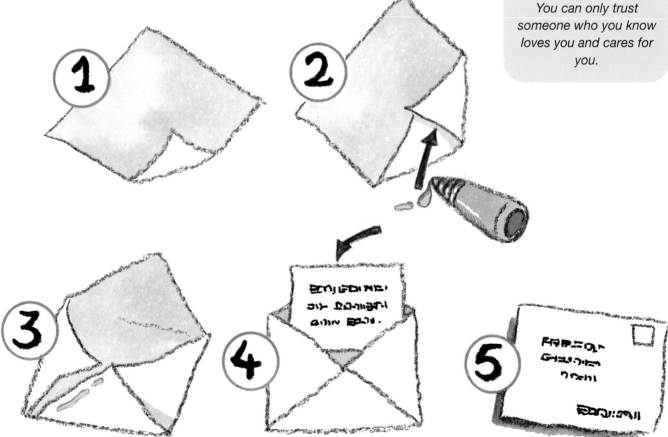

16 unselfishness

• *John 6:9*
There is a lad here, which hath five barley loaves, and two small fishes: but what are they among so many?

Jesus's disciples had to feed about five thousand people, and they didn't know how to do it. Nearby there was a young boy who had five loaves of bread and two fishes. He was willing to share what he had, and he gave it all to Jesus, who multiplied it—making it enough for everyone.

• **CHILDREN SOMETIMES SAY**
- I want the biggest piece of cake!

• **WHAT DO WE ANSWER?**
- When we have a cake, it is important to share it with everyone else. We need to think about others!

• **A FEW MINUTES TO THINK**
Children usually think about themselves first. As adults, we have to help them be generous. When we are willing to share what we have with them, our example will help them learn how to be unselfish.

Pebble soup

THE STORY

There was a soldier who came back from war, and he was starving. He hadn't eaten for days. He knocked on the doors of the houses in the town asking for food, but nobody had anything to give him to eat.

Then, he saw some children playing next to a fountain, and he went over to them. "Who are you?" the children asked. "I'm a soldier, and I have been to war. I am so hungry right now that I could eat a *pebble soup*!"

"A *pebble soup*?" the children replied. "What's that?" The soldier asked: "Does anyone have a big saucepan and a ladle?"

"We have an enormous one at home, I'll go and get it," said one of the girls. So they filled the saucepan with water from the fountain, collected pebbles, washed them, and put them inside the saucepan.

They started a big fire and stirred the soup. After a while, the soldier tasted it and said: "Mmm, it's good, but it needs a little salt." One of the boys said: "We have salt at home, I'll go and get some!"

The soldier stirred the water some more and said: "Mmm, very good, but if only we had some chicken."

Another boy said: "We have some chicken at home!" And he ran to get it.

Little by little the soldier told them what the *pebble soup* needed, and the children brought bread, chickpeas, potatoes, oil, and carrots until the soldier tasted the soup and said: "Mmm, this is an excellent *pebble soup*! Go to all the houses in town and tell everyone to bring a bowl and a spoon so that they can have some of our *pebble soup*!"

And in this way, in a town where people said there was nothing to eat and where everybody cared only about themselves, the soldier showed children how to share what little they had so that everyone had something good to eat.

This week . . .
I will share something I have with my friends by . . .

Loaves and fishes

HANDICRAFT

Material
Acetate film, a glass and paint suitable for glass or acetate film, glue.

1. Place the acetate film over the template on page 120. Paint 5 loaves of bread and 2 fishes on to the film.
2. Let them dry.
3. Cut out the fish and the loaves and glue them onto the glass.

We will remind the children that each time they see this symbol or use this glass, they should remember how important it is to share what they have with others—to be unselfish.

17 Discernment

• *Luke 20:25*
And he said unto them, Render therefore unto Cæsar the things which be Cæsar's, and unto God the things which be God's.

At the time of the Roman empire, the political authorities spread the rumor that Jesus was telling people not to pay tributes to Caesar, who was the emperor. When the Pharisees, who were a religious group, asked Jesus what they should do, Jesus said, "you should not confuse what belongs to God with what belongs to the empire."

• **CHILDREN SOMETIMES SAY**
- I am more important than my friends because I know more.

• **WHAT DO WE ANSWER?**
- Knowing things does not make a person more important.

• **A FEW MINUTES TO THINK**
Asking questions is a good way of learning. Our questions help us to see things more clearly and also to learn that it is more important to be a good person than to be intelligent!

Who Will Be first to Cross?

GAME AND HANDICRAFT

Once upon a time, there was a man walking along with a wolf, a sheep, and a cabbage. After walking for a long time, he got to a river, but there was no bridge to cross over it—only a very small boat that would only take the man and one of the animals. He wondered what he could do to get across the river with the wolf, the sheep, and the cabbage. If he left the animals behind and crossed the river, taking the cabbage with him, the wolf would eat the sheep. If he left the cabbage with the sheep, the sheep would eat the cabbage.

Do you know the answer?

You can get some help using the following cards to represent the situation.

Material
Some cardboard, markers, colored pencils, scissors.

1. Cut out 5 small pieces of cardboard and one large piece.
2. Draw and paint a river on the large card.
3. On each of the other cards, draw and paint a cabbage, a man, a wolf, a sheep, and a boat.

This week . . .
I will discern the best way to help someone by . . .

Solution:
- On the first trip across the river, the man takes the sheep across.
- On the second trip, the man takes the cabbage across to the other side, leaves it there, and takes the sheep back with him so it will not eat the cabbage.
- On the third trip, the man takes the wolf across and leaves him there with the cabbage.
- On the fourth trip, the man takes the sheep with him, and then he can continue his journey.

In this way, the man uses his intelligence to help all of them get to the other side safely.

18 openness

• *Psalm 46:8*
Come, behold the works of the Lord.

The psalmist invites us to know how great God is, to admire his works and be grateful for everything he has done for us all.

• CHILDREN SOMETIMES SAY

- I know, I know, but I only want to share what I am willing to share. I don't want my friends to play with my favorite toys! I want to choose what they can play with.

• WHAT DO WE ANSWER?

- When you ask one of your friends to come to your house to play, you must be willing to let him play with your toys. They seem more interesting because for him they are new and different.

• A FEW MINUTES TO THINK

It is hard for children to share their favorite toys. When they have visitors, it gives us the chance to help them learn to be open to their friends, to learn to please others and put their wishes first.

Who is Coming this summer?

LET'S CHAT

Imagine inviting a child from a country with few resources to spend the summer with us. Think about what we have to do to prepare for the arrival of this visitor.

- Ask the children if they are enthusiastic about the idea.
- Encourage the children to think about how good it will be to have visitors from other countries, to discover things about their culture, and to introduce them to the special things in our culture.
- Talk about having new friends.
- Prepare them for the fact that it will not always be easy. Sometimes there will be jealousy, selfishness, and rivalry. Let them talk about how to cope and the importance of being very respectful of them however different they are.
- Plan with them places to take the visitor, some activities, games, and so on.

At the end of the imagined visit, evaluate the experience with the children. Let them share how they felt. Help them recall the happy moments together and what they have learned.

Playing together

GAMES

This week . . .
I will try to remember that God loves everyone.

Find time to play some games. Games like Domino and Monopoly are fun to play. They help us

- have fun.
- learn how to follow rules.
- learn that winning is not what counts; what is important is how we play the game, how we accept losing and how ready we are to share in the happiness of the winner.

19 confiᴅence

• *Psalm 70:1*
Make haste, O God, to deliver me; make haste to help me, O Lord.

Many times, when we feel lost or in difficulty, we ask help from someone we know will lend us a hand. In this psalm, David asks the Lord to help him be confident.

• **CHILDREN SOMETIMES SAY**

- I don't want to go to the swimming pool! I am afraid I might drown!

• **WHAT DO WE ANSWER?**

- You will be safe. There will be someone there to make sure you are OK.

• **A FEW MINUTES TO THINK**

When children are afraid or feel insecure, it is important to listen to them and to talk through their fear. The psalm tells us how important it is for us to be heard, to have help when we are facing some difficulties or feel insecure.

Would you like to help me?

DRAMATIZATION

Ask the children to talk about a scenario where someone asks for help.
What would they say? Get them to talk through the problem and tell how best they could reach out to a friend in need of help.

This week . . .
I will help someone by . . .

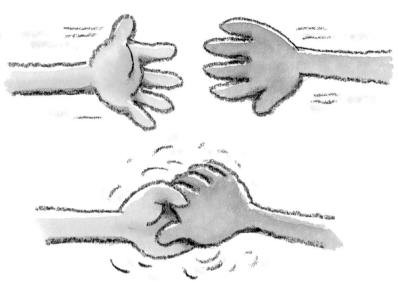

Blindfolded

GAME

Material
A handkerchief or a piece of cloth for the blindfold.

Procedure
Get a group of children to divide into groups of two so that every player has a partner. One of the children in each pair is blindfolded, and that child stands in the middle of a circle, while the others form the circle around them a few steps away. Each of the others calls the name of the blindfolded partner and guides her around without touching her.
The purpose of the game is to rely on someone to help you move around safely and with confidence.

20 communication

• *1 Samuel 3:10*
And the Lord came, and stood, and called as at other times, Samuel, Samuel. Then Samuel answered, Speak; for thy servant heareth.

Samuel was a boy who paid attention to God talking to him; he listened to God.

• **CHILDREN SOMETIMES SAY**
- Hey, listen, you know something?

• **WHAT DO WE ANSWER?**
- Please do not interrupt when we are talking.

• **A FEW MINUTES TO THINK**
It is good to be able to talk openly about what is happening to us.
But do we give one another a chance to talk?
And do we try not to interrupt conversations?
Do we wait for an answer when we ask a question?Are we prepared to accept an opinion different from ours?

Who is it?
GAME

- Each person thinks of a well-known person (a Bible character, a pop star, or a friend or relative).
- Then the other players ask questions to find out who it is.
- The answers can only be yes or no.
- The player who guesses the right name thinks of the name of the next character.

For example:
Question: Is it a woman?
Answer: Yes.
Question: Is it someone we see on television?
Answer: No.
Question: Is she alive?
Answer: Yes.

Telephone
HANDICRAFT AND GAME

Material
2 plastic cups, a few metres of string, markers or stickers for decoration, scissors, and a hole-puncher.

Procedure
1. Decorate the cups with markers or stickers.
2. Make a little hole in the base of the cups.
3. Tie a knot at one of the ends of the string.
4. Thread the string through the hole in one of the cups so the knot will remain hidden inside the cup.
5. Pass the string through the hole in the other cup, but in this case it will have to go through from the outside.
6. Tie a knot at the other end of the string. When the string is tightened, the knot will remain hidden inside the cup.

One of the players sends a message through one of the cups. The player who receives the message will pull the string tightly and put the other cup to his ear. Messages can be sent from one room to another or from downstairs to upstairs.

This week . . .
I will try to listen without interrupting when people talk to me.

COMMUNICATING
You are a good communicator if you are a good listener.

21 Discretion

• *Matthew 9:30*
And their eyes were opened; and Jesus straitly charged them, saying, See that no man know it.

When Jesus helped someone, he did not brag about it. As his followers, we should try to copy him in our behavior.

• **CHILDREN SOMETIMES SAY**

- If we go to the park and we see that poor boy I gave my bike to, I will tell him it was mine.

• **WHAT DO WE ANSWER?**

- You probably will not see him in the park, but if you do, you should not tell everybody about it. It might embarrass the boy.

• **A FEW MINUTES TO THINK**

Children say what they are thinking! We have to teach them to be careful not to say things that might hurt people's feelings without inhibiting their spontaneity and sincerity.

Cloth Printing

HANDICRAFT
With the help of an adult

Material

Cardboard, crayons that can be used on cloth, a plain piece of cloth, a hand towel, a T-shirt, pins, an iron, and a newspaper.

1. Make a drawing on the piece of cardboard using the crayons.
2. Help the child place the newspaper on the ironing board and the piece of cloth on top of the newspaper.
3. Place the drawing face down over the piece of cloth and keep it in place with pins.
4. Iron (no steam) the cardboard for a few minutes.
5. Turn up one of the corners of the cardboard a little to check if the drawing has come through.
6. The heat from the iron will fix the drawing on the cloth so that it can be washed.

WARNING
Be discreet!
Be spontaneous, but be careful not to hurt other people's feelings.

Keep a Secret!

Take the T-shirt or the hand towel you have printed and keep it in your cupboard until you are ready to give it to the person you have made it for. You may want to look at it every day, but keep it a secret from the person you are going to give it to until you are ready to give it to him or her. It is very important to be able to keep a secret!

This week . . .
I will do something good for someone, and I will not tell anyone what I have done.

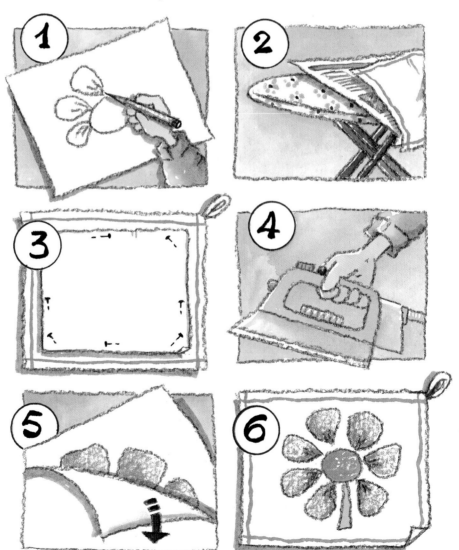

22 Environment

• *Genesis 1:28*
And God blessed them, and God said unto them . . . have dominion over the fish of the sea, and over the fowl of the air, and over every living thing that moveth upon the earth.

This value is about knowing, loving, respecting, and defending our planet.

• **CHILDREN SOMETIMES SAY**
- Look at these pretty flowers I have picked for you.

• **WHAT DO WE ANSWER?**
- Thank you, they are lovely; but we should not pick flowers every time we go out in the countryside. If everybody did the same, the countryside would have no flowers left!

• **A FEW MINUTES TO THINK**
Invite the children to talk about the way we can take care of our planet, how we should look after our fish, our birds, and our animals—all the environment around us. Make them aware of how important it is not to waste paper and water and ask the children what they know about recycling.

The smell of nature

AN OUTING

Take a walk to a park or a nearby forest. Notice the different kinds of trees, shrubs, and insects, and the path you are following. Notice, too, the smells of nature and all the different colors and textures.
Pick up some stones and plants to use to make a *nature table*.

- Notice how well the park or forest is taken care of. Think about who the park or the forest belongs to. Is it ours? Do we thank God for it?

This week . . .
I will thank God for the world around me, and I will take better care of . . .

Building an ecosystem

EXPERIMENT

Material
A fish tank, stones, some garden soil, plants, and insects.

1. Place some garden soil and some stones at the bottom of the fish tank.
2. Put in some plants.
3. When they have taken root, you can add some insects.

You can make a small aquarium if you fill the fish tank with water instead of soil. Add some stones, aquatic plants, and goldfish. You will need to take care of the ecosystem, and you might invite others in your family or in your class at school to take turns taking care of it. If you don't take care of it, it will be ruined and the insects or fish will die. Remember that an ecosystem is a community of creatures who are living in the world with us.

23 cheerfulness

• *Psalm 30:11*
Thou hast turned for me my mourning into dancing: thou hast put off my sackcloth, and girded me with gladness.

David was very sad, and he asked God for help; God cheered him up.

• **CHILDREN SOMETIMES SAY**
- I don't know what is wrong, but I'm sad and I feel like crying.

• **WHAT DO WE ANSWER?**
- Come here, then, I'll give you a hug.

• **A FEW MINUTES TO THINK**
There are times when we feel sad or worried about something. It's hard to change the way we feel and get back to being cheerful. It is like that with enthusiasm; it's easy to be enthusiastic about big things, but it is more important to be enthusiastic about the little things in life. That helps make us happy.

We enjoy . . .

LET'S CHAT

When you are with your friends, think about the little things you enjoy.

For example
- Having an ice cream.
- Watching a film together with the family while eating a pizza.
- Listening to music.
- Playing in the park on the swings.

This week . . .
I will try to think about the small things that make me happy, especially . . .

Let's Dance a Hebrew Dance

DANCE

Part A:
All the children form a circle, putting their hands on the shoulders of the children next to them, and then they move like a wheel, once to the right and then to the left.

Part B:
The children form another circle holding hands. First they take steps toward the center of the circle and then they walk back.

End:
Same as part A.

24 HOPE

• *Ephesians 1:12*
That we should be to the praise of his glory, who first trusted in Christ.

Everybody has hope in something; the people who believe in God hope to see God one day.

• **CHILDREN SOMETIMES SAY**
- Somebody I don't like sat next to me at the cinema today.

• **WHAT DO WE ANSWER?**
- Long, long ago it was unthinkable that a black person and a white person would live together. There were schools, buses, and restaurants for black people, and there were the same for whites; a black person would never go into a place exclusively for white people, and a white person would never go into a place exclusively for black people.

• **A FEW MINUTES TO THINK**
The Nobel prize winner Martin Luther King hoped that someday blacks and whites would sit together. He is famous for saying "I have a dream," and this was his dream.

- What hopes do you have?
- Do you think a child can make a difference in the world? Children have to be taught that changes start with us. If we don't want racism to exist, we must begin by accepting people of different races and treating them no differently from anyone else.

Mask-making

HANDICRAFT

Material
Cardboard, scissors, pencil and rubber, crayons, varnish, 8-inch elastic band for the mask and cotton, colored paper, scrubbing wool, and cloth for hair.

1. On each piece of cardboard, draw the face of a boy or girl from different races, making sure all of them are represented. Go to pages 114 and 115 for ideas.
2. Color them with the crayons and apply a coating of varnish.
3. Make holes for the eyes.
4. Punch a little hole at both sides of the face, pass the ends of the elastic band through the holes, and tie a knot at each end.
5. Fix the hair onto the sides of the mask with the cotton.

The Chair game

GAME

Material
A stereo, chairs (one less than the number of participants), the masks.

How to play
- Someone starts and stops the music.
- Chairs are placed in the middle of the circle formed by the children.
- When the music starts, the players begin walking around the chairs.
- When the music stops, all the players try to sit down, and the player who cannot find a chair to sit on is out of the game.
- Each time a child goes out, a chair is removed and the circle becomes smaller.
- The winner is the player who sits in the last chair available.

To play this game you will wear the masks because noone can see who you are behind the masks. You are all the same.
We hope that one day all people will befriend one another—no matter what their color, their nationality, their language, their religion, or their social differences are.

This week . . .
I will befriend someone who is different from me.

SAYVILLE LIBRARY

25 Sincerity

• *Proverbs 11:20*
They that are of a froward heart are abomination to the Lord: but such as are upright in their way are his delight.

God wants us to be honest, sincere, spontaneous, and frank.

• **CHILDREN SOMETIMES SAY**
- I have lost my watch! I am so sorry! I know you told me not to take it to school.

• **WHAT DO WE ANSWER?**
- You should have done what you were told, but it is good that you are able to say you are sorry.

• **A FEW MINUTES TO THINK**
Sincerity is an important attitude to have, and we need to encourage children to be sincere.

A Personal Diary

HANDICRAFT

Material

White and colored sheets of paper, cardboard from a box, scissors, permanent marker, hole puncher, printed cloth, glue, and some ribbon.

1. Cut two sides of the cardboard box the same size as the sheets of paper. They will be the covers.

2. Place one cover on top and the other under the sheets of paper, and punch the holes on one of the sides.
3. Cut out two pieces of cloth, bigger than the covers.
4. Apply some glue to the covers and press them on the cloth. Fold the remaining cloth inside the cover. Line the inside of each cover with a colored sheet of paper for a nice finishing touch.
5. Once the covers are lined with the cloth, put the white sheets of paper between them.
6. Pass the ribbon through the holes, and tie with a bow.
7. Write MY DIARY on the top cover using a marker. Or you can stick a label with your name on it to the cover.

Your diary is a place where you can write down how you feel and what happens to you. It is a place where you can be sincere, and this will help you to learn about being sincere with others too.

DIARY

If you are sincere in your diary, it will help you remember when you are older how you felt about things when you were younger.

This week . . .
I will be sincere with someone about how I feel.

WEEK

26 Generosity

• *Proverbs 11:17*
The merciful man doeth good to his own soul: but he that is cruel troubleth his own flesh.

The generous person is the one who thinks of others, the one who helps without expecting anything back, the one who can forgive without resentment. Generosity does not make distinctions; generosity opens our hearts and enriches us.

• **CHILDREN SOMETIMES SAY**
- I left my sandwich behind, but my friend gave me some of his, and it was very good.

• **WHAT DO WE ANSWER?**
- Your friend was generous! It is not easy to share your food when you are hungry. I hope you will do the same for other friends if they leave their food behind.

• **A FEW MINUTES TO THINK**
Together with the children, think about a time when they were generous. You will probably have many examples. Don't only give examples of generosity from a material point of view. Try to encourage them to think about other types of generosity, such as forgiveness or inviting children who are left out to join them at play time.

A generous tree

THE STORY

Once upon a time, there was a tree that loved a boy very much, and the boy loved the tree. The boy used leaves from the tree to make crowns, he climbed up the trunk and used the branches as swings, he ate the apples that grew on the tree, and when he was tired, he sat down at the foot of the tree and fell asleep. The tree was happy. When the boy grew up, he stopped doing all these things because he said he was too old for that and he needed money. "Can you give me money?" he asked the tree. "Pick my apples and sell them" the tree replied. The boy did so, and the tree was happy. Time passed. The boy did not come to visit, and the tree was sad. One day the boy came back, but he did not want to swing from the branches. He said: "I want to have children and a house. Can you give me that?" "Take my branches and build your house with them," replied the tree. The young man did so, and the tree was happy. Time passed, and the young man became a grown man. Once again, the tree was sad because he did not go to see it. One day the man came back, but he did not climb up the trunk. "I want to have a boat and travel. Can you give me that?" he said. "Cut my trunk and build your boat," said the tree. The man did so, and the tree was happy. Time passed, and the man became an old man. The tree was sad because the old man did not go to see him. Finally, one day the old man came back, and the tree told him, "I'm sorry, I would like to give you something, but I have nothing left." "I don't need many things now; I only need a quiet place to rest," the man said. "I still have a stump left. You can lean against that and get some rest," replied the tree. The old man did so, and it made the tree very, very happy.

Let's make a puppet theater

HANDICRAFT—DRAMATIZATION

Material

A shoebox without a lid, some cardboard, tracing paper, templates from pages 116–119, cutter and scissors, black pencil, colored pencils, cloth, and glue.
Decoration: a tree
Characters: a boy, a young man, a man, an old man (always the same person)
Fittings: apples, branches, trunk, house, and boat.

1. Cut out a very narrow rectangle on the wider side of th box and slide in the background decoration (as in the picture).
2. Cut a very narrow rectangle on the narrower side and slide in the characters.
3. Print out or trace, paint, and cut out the templates.
4. Cut out a piece of cloth to make the curtain.
5. Glue it where the illustration indicates.
6. Read the story "A generous tree" and stage it.

This week . . .
I will be generous by . . .

WEEK

27 Gratitude

• *Philippians 1:3*
I thank my God upon every remembrance of you.

When the apostle Paul wrote these words, he was in prison. Paul had always appreciated the people who helped him, and in this letter addressed to the Philippians, he expressed his deep gratitude to them because they had helped him every time he needed it.

• **CHILDREN SOMETIMES SAY**
- Thank you for doing me a big favor!

• **WHAT DO WE ANSWER?**
- You are welcome! I hope you will remember to do a favor for someone else who needs it!

• **A FEW MINUTES TO THINK**
Gratitude is a value that we learn. We can help children learn this value by giving them a good example. It is worth thinking about whether we always say thank you and about whether we are thankful for the way we are and for what we have.

We give thanks

LET'S CHAT

Each member of the group is invited to talk about a time when they needed help. They are then invited to remember how they gave thanks for the help received. They might make a list of different ways they express their gratitude.

For example:
- I say thank you with a kiss or a hug.
- I write a thank you letter or email.
- I visit the person, perhaps taking a gift.

This week . . .
I will think of the things I am grateful for.

Let's make an acrostic

GAME

Write a word vertically and think about words starting with each of the letters in the word. Follow the example with the word LOVE.

L istening
O bedience
V alues
E nvironment

Write more acrostics with other words; you may even use a dictionary to help you find them.

WEEK

28 Honesty

• *Proverbs 16:8*
Better is a little with righteousness than great revenues without right.

The proverb tells us to be honest and to earn things honestly.

• **CHILDREN SOMETIMES SAY**
- John got a good grade on his math test, but he copied from Ann and the teacher never realized it!

• **WHAT DO WE ANSWER?**
- What John did was not honest, and it will not help John. If he did not understand how to do the math problems, he should have told the teacher. Then the teacher could have explained them to him and he would have been able to do the exam without cheating.

• **A FEW MINUTES TO THINK**
Cheating can bring immediate results, and it is hard for children to realize that it is wrong to cheat. We always hear of people who get rich by cheating other people. But is it good? Does it make us happy?

Making Bags
HANDICRAFT—EXPERIMENT

Material
Pieces of cloth (plain or otherwise), scissors, needle and thread, string, scales, markers, labels, sand, and coins.

1. Write different values on each label, for example honesty, wisdom, and patience.
2. Make a few bags with the cloth.
3. Fill them with sand, weigh them, and attach a label.
4. Put the bags on one of the trays of the scales and a few coins or a silver ring on the other. (The small bags should weigh a little more.)
5. Which tray of the scales would you choose? Why?
6. Think about the heavier tray.

In life, values such as honesty hold more weight than all the money in the world.

This week . . .
I will think about ways I can act more honestly.

Two stalls at the market
DRAMATIZATION

Material
2 tables, 2 scales, 2 baskets, toy coins, and things to sell, for example fruit, toys, noodles, and vegetables.

In one of the stalls, there will be an honest shop assistant. In the other market stall, there will be a shop assistant who cheats.

The honest shop assistant must act honestly in all situations, making sure that she charges the customer the right price and gives the right change. The dishonest shop assistant acts dishonestly, cheating the customers and giving too little change or charging too much. There may be cases when the customers do not realize they are being cheated; but when they do, how do they react? How do the shop assistants prove they are honest?
The children can take turns being the shop assistant and the customers.

29 Justice

- *Proverbs 14:34*
Righteousness exalteth a nation: but sin is a reproach to any people.

Solomon tells us that a just nation is one that allows all of its members to have the same opportunities. If we want to be proud of our people, we must work with justice.

- **CHILDREN SOMETIMES SAY**
- On TV they said farmers were on strike because they were paid very little for the fruit they produce. But we hear people complaining fruit is very expensive. Is that right?

- **WHAT DO WE ANSWER?**
- Farmers are badly paid for their products sometimes and they are right to complain. A product sometimes becomes more expensive in the marketing process (transport, storage, distribution, and the sale to markets or supermarkets).

- **A FEW MINUTES TO THINK**
You can tell children about fair shops where you are sure that you are paying a fair price for a product, where no one in the process takes more than their fair share.
Children understand the concept of justice, but sometimes they do not apply it correctly. For example, if somebody has hurt them and you ask them what the punishment should be, the answer could be unreasonable. Likewise, children sometimes think that their parents or teachers are unfair in the way they treat them. It is good to help them understand justice from different points of view.

Let's go shopping

AN OUTING

At a fair shop
- Make a list of the products on sale.
- Write down the price of each product.
- Buy a bar of chocolate.

At a supermarket
- Look for the same products, although they will have different brand names.
- Write down the price of each product.
- Buy a bar of chocolate.

ACTING JUSTLY
*To be just
is to treat
all people fairly.*

Sweet talk

LET'S CHAT

Ask the children to break the two bars of chocolate into small pieces and put each kind in a separate dish.

- Is there a difference in price in the products bought at one shop or the other?
- Why are the products from one of the shops more expensive?
- Does advertising have something to do with the difference in price?
- What can we do?

When you have finished discussing this, close or blindfold your eyes, take a piece of chocolate from each dish, and eat it.

- Can you notice any difference between the two pieces of chocolate?

This week . . .
I will go to a fair shop and buy . . .

30 Diligence

- **Ecclesiastes 5:12**

The sleep of a labouring man is sweet, whether he eat little or much: but the abundance of the rich will not suffer him to sleep.

A good worker is a person who enjoys doing his job and feels satisfied when it is finished.

- **CHILDREN SOMETIMES SAY**
- I spent all afternoon tidying the drawers in my room.

- **WHAT DO WE ANSWER?**
- Very good! You have worked really hard, and now you will be able to find what you are looking for and also have the satisfaction of having a nice, tidy room.

- **A FEW MINUTES TO THINK**

Let's think about difficult jobs and what it is like to stick at the job.
- In the end, does it bring us satisfaction?
- What else can it bring us?

A mosaic
HANDICRAFT

Material
Wooden base, approximately, 8 x 8 in; small mosaic stones; dry beans or soup noodles; glue; paper; pencil or marker; varnish.

1. Draw a picture on a sheet of paper. At first it is better to choose something simple.
2. Glue the picture to the wooden base.
3. Glue the small, colored stones into the different spaces in the picture. If you use beans or soup noodles, you may want to paint them first. Remember to apply some varnish afterwards or the stones may fall off.

You will find some ideas for your mosaics on page 123.

Working hard
HELPING OUT

Try helping with some household chores or with some small tasks at school. For example
- Setting and clearing the table.
- Doing the dishes.
- Keeping your papers and your desk tidy.
- Emptying the waste basket.
- Being responsible for putting things into the recycling bins.

You can find a thousand ways to help both at home and at school every day. Everyone should be ready to help a little.

This week . . .
I will help out at home or at school by doing . . .

31 Freedom

• *Galatians 5:13*
For, brethren, ye have been called unto liberty; only use not liberty for an occasion to the flesh, but by love serve one another.

The apostle Paul calls the Jewish people to be free—free to be responsible, free to be without envy, without jealousy or rivalry.

• **CHILDREN SOMETIMES SAY**
-   We are going on a school outing tomorrow, but the teacher told us we have to do as we are told. That's not freedom!

• **WHAT DO WE ANSWER?**
-   Doing what you want does not mean you are free; when you go on a school outing, you must be careful and responsible.

• **A FEW MINUTES TO THINK**
Sometimes children think that freedom means that they should be unrestrained.
If our freedom does not respect our neighbors, then it is not freedom.
Freedom goes hand in hand with responsibility. If we think something is good for ourselves but not for everybody else, then it is not good for us either.

A "flying" game
HANDICRAFT—SURPRISE

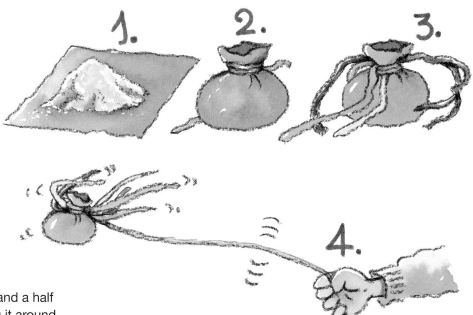

Material
String, squares of cloth 4 x 4 in, strips of tissue paper or cloth in different colors about a foot long, sawdust or sand.

1. Put a spoonful of sand in the center of each piece of cloth.
2. Pick up the four corners and tie them together.
3. Tie the strips of tissue paper with the same string.
4. The string should be between a foot and a half and 2 feet long so that you can swing it around.

If you swing it hard enough, it will fly away, but be careful not to hit anyone! You should play this game outside.

Playing with water
EXPERIMENT

This activity is divided into two parts, and it is a fun activity.

Material
Glasses (one per person), 2 or 3 buckets, water, and a floor mop for spilled water.

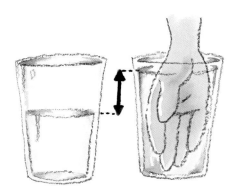

First part
1. Half fill the glasses with water.
2. Play with the water inside the glass, keeping your fingers inside the glass.
3. You are not allowed to spill any water. The player who does spill some water is out.
4. This activity can last about 5 minutes.

Second part
1. Half fill the buckets with water.
2. Splash around in the water, keeping your hands inside the bucket.
3. Again, no water should be spilled, and if it is, it has to be mopped up.
4. This activity can last longer than the previous one.

- Which activity was more fun?
- Which activity restricted you more?
- Both activities had rules; but which activity helped you to be more responsible?

This week . . .
I will choose to be free to . . .

32 OBEDIENCE

• *Genesis 6:22*
Thus did Noah; according to all that God commanded him, so did he.

Noah was pleased to obey, and God rewarded him.

● **CHILDREN SOMETIMES SAY**

- I'm coming, I'm coming! Just a minute!

● **WHAT DO WE ANSWER?**

- How many times do you have to be called? Please come now!

● **A FEW MINUTES TO THINK**

Children find it difficult to obey immediately! They find it hard to leave the game they are playing or the TV program they are watching, and sometimes we have to tell them many times before they listen and obey. Ask them if they think they do what they are told immediately. Ask them what happens if they do obey. We are going to listen to the story of Noah. Think about how different the story would have been if he had not obeyed immediately.

Noah and his ark

THE STORY

Many, many years ago, there lived a man called Noah. He was a good person, just and obedient, and he always trusted God. At that time, there were people in the world who would only think about doing wrong. God was sad and told Noah, "I am going to send a great flood, and everybody will drown. The earth is full of violence because of these people. I want you to make an ark with cypress wood, three stories high, with a window half a meter from the roof and a door on the side. I want you to get into the ark with your family. In addition, you should bring a male and female from every species and food and drinking supplies."

Noah did what God told him; and, when the ark was full, the flood began. It rained for forty days and forty nights. The earth was flooded with water. After forty days, the sun came out and Noah let a dove fly out of the window. The bird flew back with a twig from an olive tree in its beak. Noah knew that the flood was over. A few days later, the water was back in place and the ground was dry. The people and the animals left the ark and multiplied.

This week...
I will do my best to be obedient.

A model

HANDICRAFT
With the help of an adult

Material
Modeling clay in different colors, a big box made of cardboard or wood, 3 small rectangular boxes in different sizes, glue, paint and brushes, tools for modeling, and scissors or cutter.

1. Model Noah and pairs of different animals out of modeling clay.
2. For the ark, glue the three cardboard boxes together, one on top of the other and, with the help of an adult, make a window and a door as indicated in the story (and in the illustration).
3. Paint the ark.
4. Paint the sky and the ground on two pieces of paper.
5. Glue them to the inside of the bigger box, so it will look like a small theater.
6. Place all the plastic putty figures inside the small theater.

According to the number of people, you can tell the whole story of Noah and his ark with several different models.

33 Patience

• *Proverbs 15:18*
A wrathful man stirreth up strife: but he that is slow to anger appeaseth strife.

It is better to be at peace than to be a worrier.

• **CHILDREN SOMETIMES SAY**
- Some children laughed at me today, calling me small and skinny, but I did not pay any attention to them.

• **WHAT DO WE ANSWER?**
- Well done. They only want you to get upset. If you are patient, they will leave you alone. But if you argue with them, they will just keep bothering you.

• **A FEW MINUTES TO THINK**
It is hard to know what to say to a child in this situation. We wonder if the child was being patient or if he had just become resigned to being treated like that. Patience is an active virtue. It requires an effort; it is not being passive. We must help our children be patient.

Let's go fishing
HANDICRAFT

Material
Buckets, water, wooden or plastic sticks, fishing thread, string, paper clips, pieces of cork, templates (page 121), hard transparent plastic, markers, permanent markers, cleaning rag, scissors, hole puncher.

The fish
1. Draw the outline of the fish with nonpermanent markers on the plastic; if you make a mistake, you can rub it out with a rag.
2. Color the fish with the permanent markers and cut them out.
3. Make a hole in the upper part so you can catch them.
4. Cut the pieces of cork into rectangular shapes.
5. Make a deep cut in each piece of cork to insert the fish.

The fishing rods
1. Tie the fishing thread to the end of each stick.
2. Attach an open paper clip to the end of each thread.

Fill the bucket with water. Put your fish in the water and you are ready to go fishing.

If you write the numbers from 1 to 9 at the bottom of each cork, you can add up the numbers of the fish you have caught and the player with the most points will be the winner.

This week...
I will try to be patient.

WEEK 34

peace

• *Matthew 5:9*
Blessed are the peacemakers: for they shall be called the children of God.

Working toward peace is working to achieve a society free of hatred, resentment, and injustice. The person who works for peace is happy because she is working for the happiness of other people.

• **CHILDREN SOMETIMES SAY**
- This ball is mine! Someone else says, "No, it's mine! I found it, so it belongs to me!"

• **WHAT DO WE ANSWER?**
- Let's have some peace here! If you both share the ball, you will both have fun; but if only one of you has the ball, it's not fair.

• **A FEW MINUTES TO THINK**
Peace is so easily lost. Pride, power, and ambition almost always bring conflicts. We should work together and share what we have if we want a world full of peace and happiness.

The Peace Dove
HANDICRAFT AND SONG

Material

Chalk or paint, paper approximately 6.5 x 6.5 ft, tea candles.

1. Draw a peace dove on paper or on the ground using chalk or paint.
2. Place lighted candles around the outline of the dove.
3. Each member of the group will say aloud the verse from Matthew 5:9 "Blessed are the peacemakers" in a different tone of voice: sad, happy, in song...

Blowing the feather
GAME

This is a game for two or more players. It consists of keeping a feather up in the air by blowing it so it will not fall to the ground. The same game can be played with a balloon, but you keep the balloon in the air using your hands.

When you play games like this, you work together to keep the feather or the balloon in the air. It helps you to realize how much fun you can have when you cooperate with one another, avoiding conflicts and competitiveness.

This week . . .
I will think of ways I can be a peacemaker.

35 Integrity

• *Matthew 7:20*
Wherefore by their fruits ye shall know them.

If we look at fruit trees in the early spring, we see only their leaves. We probably don't know whether they are pear trees, apple trees, or cherry trees. But if we see the same trees in the summertime, we will see the fruit growing on the trees, and we will see what kind of trees they are.
People are also recognized by their "fruits"—that is, by everything they do, whether good or bad.

• **CHILDREN SOMETIMES SAY**

- I don't want to cry, but some films make me cry. Do you think people will call me a crybaby if they see me crying?

• **WHAT DO WE ANSWER?**

- There is nothing wrong with crying. It shows you have feelings.

• **A FEW MINUTES TO THINK**
Crying at a sad film shows what a person is like. Sometimes we are embarrassed and we are afraid that people will think we are weak. It is good to help children express their feelings and to realize that feelings are neither bad nor good. It is an opportunity to help them accept themselves as they are and not feel ashamed of the way they feel.

What kind of tree is this?

AN OUTING—EXPERIMENT

Go to the country and collect leaves from different fruit trees. It's easier to do this in the summertime when the trees are laden with fruit since it will be easier to recognize them.

Nature Book
1. Place the leaves inside old newspaper to dry and put a weight on top so they will be well pressed.
2. When the leaves are dry, use some transparent plastic to attach each leaf to a page in your notebook.
3. Write the name of the tree and, if you want, draw and paint the fruit.
4. Write on the notebook cover "My Nature Book."
5. Every time you go into the country you can find more things to put in your nature book.

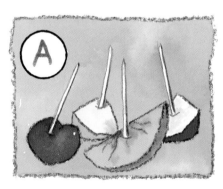

Chocolate fruits

COOKING
With the help of an adult

Ingredients
7 oz of chocolate with 70 percent cocoa, fruits (strawberries, grapes, bananas, cherries, and oranges), nuts (almonds, walnuts, hazelnuts).

Utensils
Dish, plate, two saucepans (one bigger, one smaller), spatula, cocktail sticks.

1. Put a cocktail stick into each small pieces of fruit (sliced or whole, depending on size) and put on a dish.
2. Crumble the chocolate and put it in the smaller saucepan.
3. Boil some water in the bigger saucepan.
4. Put the smaller saucepan with the crumbled chocolate inside.
5. Stir the chocolate with the spatula until it is melted.
6. Very carefully, get the adult to help you take the smaller saucepan out of the bigger one and turn off the heat.
7. Hold the pieces of fruit with the cocktail stick and dip them in the melted chocolate.
8. Let them cool on a plate in the fridge.

Which fruit are you eating now?

This week...
I will be aware of the fruits of the people in my life and thank God for them.

36 Loyalty

• *Ecclesiastes 5:4*
When thou vowest a vow unto God, defer not to pay it; for he hath no pleasure in fools: pay that which thou hast vowed.

In olden times, the word "given" was very important. If two people gave their word about something, there was no need for documents because the word they had given was enough. This verse from Ecclesiastes tells us that if we are not sure of what we promise, it is better not to promise it at all because a promise should always be kept.

• **CHILDREN SOMETIMES SAY**
- When you come to pick me up from my friend's house, I will be ready to leave. I promise.

• **WHAT DO WE ANSWER?**
- Last time you made the same promise; but you were not ready when I came and we missed our train home.

• **A FEW MINUTES TO THINK**
Children make promises very easily. At the time, they are often sincere; they want to keep their promise and they are sure they can. It is important that they learn to keep promises. Help them to make easy promises that they can keep and, in time, they will be able to make bigger and more complex promises. It sometimes helps to say to them, "Why not say, 'I'll try' instead of 'I promise,' since that is more manageable." And instead of promising something "forever," suggest they say they will promise "for a few days." This will help them learn how to make and keep promises.

A ring

HANDICRAFT

Material

Plastic beads, elastic fishing thread, small noodles with holes, markers, thread, a needle, and tape.

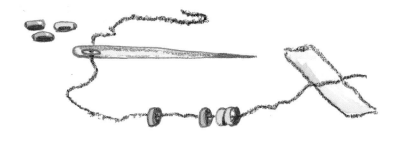

1. If you cannot find plastic beads, use noodles instead and paint them using markers of different colors.
2. Pass a piece of fishing thread through the eye of the needle.
3. Use some tape to fix one of the ends of the thread to the table where you are working.
4. Thread the plastic beads or the noodles.
5. Tie the thread to fit a finger.

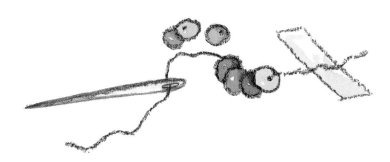

You can give this ring to a friend as a promise of friendship.

A loyalty game

GAME

Material

Paper, envelopes, a pen, and a dice.

1. Appoint a secretary.
2. Each player will have a number from 1 to 6.
3. Write tasks that can be done on a piece of paper and put the paper in an envelope.
4. Place the envelopes in the center of the table and mix them up.
5. Throw the dice. The player who has the corresponding number has to do the task described in the envelope.
6. The group secretary reads out the tasks, and they will have to be done.
The player who does not do the task is out of the game.

This week...
I promise I will ...

Some examples of tasks:
- Untie the shoelaces of all the players and then tie them up again.
- Sing a song.
- Perform some trick.

37 PRUDENCE

• *Proverbs 2:11*
Discretion shall preserve thee, understanding shall keep thee.

Prudence is a virtue. We should think about what we say and do before we say or do it. Prudence helps us act more sensibly.

• **CHILDREN SOMETIMES SAY**
- Cyclists don't have to follow the traffic rules! If they are careful, they can go even when there is a red light, can't they?

• **WHAT DO WE ANSWER?**
- Nobody should go through a red light; we all have to respect the traffic rules.

• **A FEW MINUTES TO THINK**
It is not always easy to be prudent! Sometimes we are impulsive and we don't think of the consequences of what we are doing; sometimes we are in a hurry or we are showing off. We don't understand the dangers we are putting ourselves in.
The proverb says it all: prudence will guide you, and understanding will protect you!

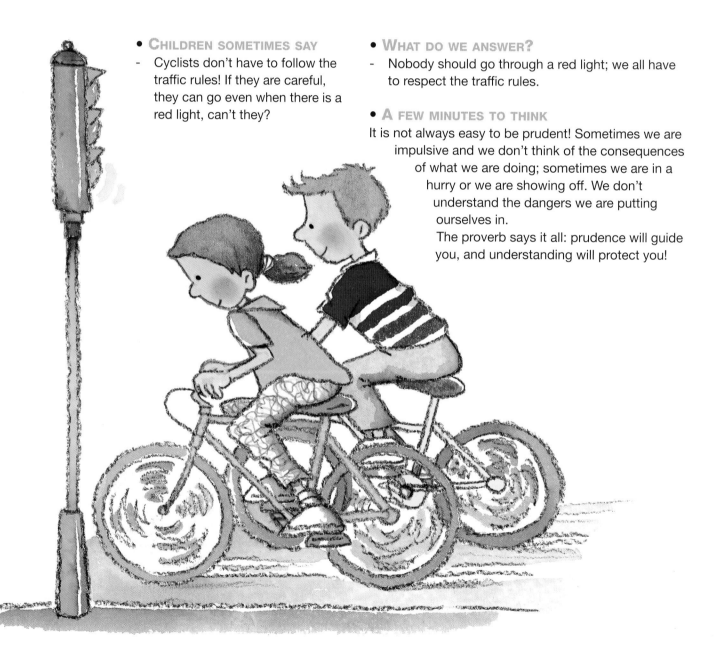

A traffic light
HANDICRAFT

Material
A sheet of long, yellow cardboard, some green, red, and yellow glossy paper, scissors, glue, hole puncher, string, and clothes pegs.

1. Fold the cardboard in half, as shown in the picture.
2. Draw the traffic light on one of the sides of the cardboard (see model on page 122).
3. Cut three circles out of the cardboard – one for each light of the traffic lights.
4. Open the folded cardboard and glue the green, red and yellow glossy paper in the appropriate holes.
5. Put some glue on the inside of the traffic light and press the front of the cardboard over the back.
6. Punch a hole at the top of the traffic light and tie a string large enough to go around a doorknob.

You can hang the traffic light from the doorknob of any door. To say "Do Not Enter!," put a clothes peg on the red circle. If people can come into the room, put a clothes peg on the green circle. If you are in the middle of doing something and you want people to be prudent when they come into the room, put a peg on the yellow circle. You can make as many traffic lights as there are rooms in the house.

SIGNS

This week...
I will try to be prudent when I...

Take notice of signs so that you can respect others and behave more sensibly.

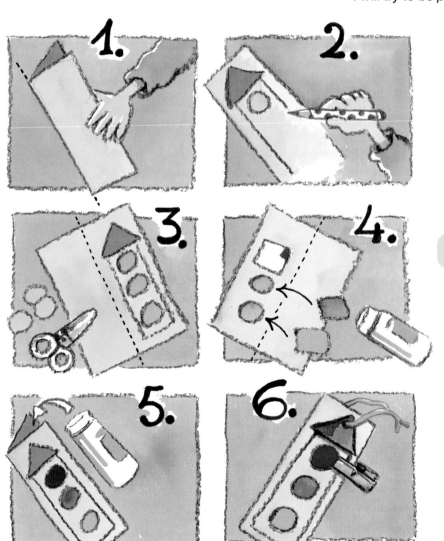

Who saw it?
LET'S CHAT

It is good to talk with children about the importance of being prudent. If you saw someone doing something imprudent, it is worth mentioning it. We can learn from other people's experiences. If there was an accident, you might ask what would have happened if the people involved had been more prudent.
When we understand the consequences of the chances we take, it helps us to be more prudent.

38 ReliaBility

• *James 5:12*
But above all things, my brethren, swear not, neither by heaven, neither by the earth, neither by any other oath: but let your yea be yea; and your nay, nay; lest ye fall into condemnation.

When someone asks us to do something, we should think carefully before saying "yes" or "no," and we should mean what we say!

• **CHILDREN SOMETIMES SAY**
- Today the teacher asked if anyone could bring some fruit to school, and I said I would.

• **WHAT DO WE ANSWER?**
- Good for you! Now don't forget because the teacher is relying on you. Why don't you put the fruit with your school bag now to remind you?

• **A FEW MINUTES TO THINK**
Reliability is an important quality. It has to do with our work, our commitments, our behavior. People need to know they can rely on us. Adults need to know they can rely on children to do their homework and to behave well in public places; children need to know they can rely on adults when they promise to do things.
Do we think before we say "yes" or "no" to a child?

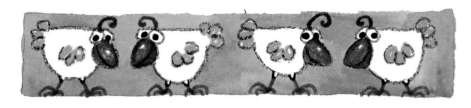

IDEAS
Here are some suggestions for decorating your "I will be reliable" signs.

Decorated Signs

HANDICRAFT

Material
Cardboard, markers and paints, brushes, hole puncher, ribbon.

1. Write the title "I will be reliable" on the cardboard.
2. Add some examples of reliability on the cardboard using the conversation from *A few minutes to think*.
Examples:
   • at work, at school, or at home
   • with your friends
3. Decorate the cardboard with a trimming or a stencil.
4. Make two holes in the upper side of the cardboard.
5. Pass the ribbon through the holes and tie a knot so that you can hang your sign in a place where you can see it and it can remind you of your promises.

Organizing a Play

ORGANIZATION—DRAMATIZATION

1. Suggest that the children organize a play.
2. Get them to plan the play by
   • Choosing the story to act out.
   • Deciding who will play each part.
   • Selecting appropriate music.
   • Making up a program.
   • Making entrance tickets.
   • Appointing an usher, a sound technician, and an MC.

3. Say that you are relying on them to do their very best!

This week...
I promise to be reliable in all I agree to do.

WEEK

39 Forgiveness

• *Matthew 6:12*
And forgive us our debts, as we forgive our debtors.

When we forgive, we should forget and not hold a grudge.

• **CHILDREN SOMETIMES SAY**

- I bumped my friend by accident and now he says he doesn't want to be my friend anymore!

• **WHAT DO WE ANSWER?**

- If you explain that it was an accident and ask him to forgive you, I hope he will understand and forgive you. Then you can be friends again.

• **A FEW MINUTES TO THINK**

Children have to learn to be forgiving and to be reconciled with one another. Even when they think it is not their fault, it is good to make up with someone. Otherwise, there are bad feelings and friendships are broken.

I'm upset

LET'S CHAT

Talk about the following scenarios and ask the children how they would react.

Invite them to talk about whether they would be forgiving and reconciling in each scenario.

1. Your friend has just taken and eaten your ice cream.
2. You are playing with a ball, and someone takes it and throws it over the fence.
3. You bump someone accidentally and they get very angry with you and say they don't want to be friends with you anymore.
4. While in a tantrum, your friend tears some sheets of paper that belong to you.

Just fiction

DRAMATIZATION

Act out the four scenarios from *I'm upset*.

This week . . .
I will try to be more forgiving.

WEEK

40 Solidarity

• *Acts 4:32*
And the multitude of them that believed were of one heart and of one soul: neither said any of them that ought of the things which he possessed was his own; but they had all things common.

The first Christians lived together, and everything they had was for the benefit of all. Many of them, like Barnabas (who owned a field) sold their possessions and gave all their money to the community.

• **CHILDREN SOMETIMES SAY**
- Why are these street musicians asking for money? Are they poor?

• **WHAT DO WE ANSWER?**
- Street musicians love to play their music, and they hope it will make people happy and then they will give them some money. It may be that they don't have a job and they need money to live. We can help them a little by giving them some money.

• **A FEW MINUTES TO THINK**
When we talk about solidarity, children may be able to give a lot of examples, but it may be more helpful to talk about being in solidarity with others, as this will help us to talk about the right attitude to have.

We show solidarity when we
• Visit a friend who is homebound.
• Take an elderly person for a walk.
• Help someone in class who is having difficulty.
• Take care of the environment around us.

Do we show solidarity when we
• Leave our plates on the table?
• Do not keep our things tidy?
• Just think of ourselves?

Let's Party

A PARTY

Why don't you organize a party at home or in your class and invite each member of the group to bring something to eat?

SHARING
At this party, everybody can share the food and then share the work of clearing the table and washing up.

A thousand ways to help

LET'S CHAT

Invite the children to talk about solidarity and how they can help one another.

Examples:
- If parents are working very hard, everyone in the family can help to prepare the food, set the table, and wash the dishes.
- If someone is in difficulty, everyone tries to find a way to help.
- If a friend at school has forgotten a book, a child can share.
- If there is a lot of litter in the playground, everyone can pick it up and throw it away.

This week . . .
I will try to show solidarity by . . .

41 Reflectiveness

• *Proverbs 16:23*
The heart of the wise teacheth his mouth, and addeth learning to his lips.

Reflectiveness is to take time to think something over. This is sometimes difficult because it requires time and space.
The writer of this proverb tells us that wise people take some time to think before they speak. They reflect on what they are going to say, and so they are more effective when they speak.

• **CHILDREN SOMETIMES SAY**
- 11 + 5 = . . . 23!

• **WHAT DO WE ANSWER?**
- Don't rush! Think before you answer.

• **A FEW MINUTES TO THINK**
Children often rush to give an answer or to say what they are thinking. We should encourage them to think before they speak. We cannot ask them to think if we don't teach them to do so or if we don't create the right atmosphere. It's important that they see that we also take the time to think before we speak. Our example speaks volumes.

Watching a film

DISCUSSION GROUP

Choose a film or a TV series for children such as *Bambi*, *Dumbo*, or any other that offers an opportunity to reflect on different situations.

For example, if we choose the film about Dumbo, we can reflect on

- Mockery (when other mother elephants laugh at Dumbo).
- Loneliness (when Dumbo's mother is isolated from Dumbo).
- Self-acceptance (when Dumbo sees that he can fly).
- The fact that we are all different (when the other elephants do not accept Dumbo because of his big ears).
- Love (Dumbo's mother loves him with his physical defect).

Quiet music

LISTENING

Choose some music and create a quiet atmosphere. Sit in a comfortable chair or, if possible, lie on the floor; avoid bright lights (natural daylight best) and play the music softly. (Any classical music might be appropriate or even modern music or instrumental music.)

This week . . .
I will think before I speak!

A MOMENT OF REFLECTION
Think!
Then reply!

42 Respect

• *1 Peter 3:15*
But sanctify the Lord God in your hearts: and be ready always to give an answer to every man that asketh you a reason of the hope that is in you with meekness and fear.

In ancient Greece, people were considered to be intelligent when they were able to defend their ideas respectfully, having pondered them in a reflective way.

• **CHILDREN SOMETIMES SAY**
- Why is the man in the green car so angry?

• **WHAT DO WE ANSWER?**
- Because the white car ran into his car and he is upset. But even if somebody runs into your car, you have to be respectful to them; it probably was an accident.

• **A FEW MINUTES TO THINK**
Respect is a fundamental principle of living together. If we want to be respected, we have to respect other people too. Indeed, we must respect people, animals, nature, and material things, and we should be careful about the way we say and do things.

Agreeing
GAME

The children are invited to imagine they are the crew on a ship leaving on a discovery trip to an unknown part of the world. Due to overbooking, there is one crew member too many. The game is about deciding who cannot get on the ship.

How can this be done?

Procedure

Before you start, remind the players it is necessary to be respectful and listen to what everyone has to say.

1. Choose a moderator.
2. Individually or by couples, choose a profession. Each crew member has to justify the need for his profession during the trip using all possible arguments.
3. The group has to debate how to rank the professions according to their importance.
4. A voting system is agreed on, and the player who represents the profession least needed for the trip will be the crew member who will remain behind.

Knock, knock! May I come in?

HANDICRAFT

Material

Cardboard, markers or colored pencils, string, hole puncher, and scissors.

1. Cut out pieces of cardboard any size you wish.
2. Write a notice saying: "Quiet! I'm studying" or "Quiet! I'm sleeping."
3. Paint the signs.
4. Make a couple of holes at the top of the signs.
5. Tie a piece of string through each hole, and the signs will be ready to hang from doorknobs.

This week . . .
I will be more respectful by . . .

43 ResponsiBility

• *Deuteronomy 31:8*
And the Lord, he it is that doth go before thee; he will be with thee, he will not fail thee, neither forsake thee.

When Moses grew old, he no longer was the guide for the people of Israel. The new guide would be Joshua. Moses told Joshua not to fear because the Lord would be with him and would not leave him.

• **CHILDREN SOMETIMES SAY**
- I think I left my jumper at school.

• **WHAT DO WE ANSWER?**
- When you go to school tomorrow, go and look for it. If you can't find it, ask your teacher. You have to be responsible for your belongings!

• **A FEW MINUTES TO THINK**
It is important to be responsible in many areas:
• Doing homework.
• Being polite.
• Taking care of one's belongings.
• Helping out at home and in some small tasks at school.

We have to help children develop a responsible attitude; teachers and families should be their role models.

Personal Diary

AN EXERCISE OF RESPONSIBILITY

Material

A notebook and a pen.

The objective of the exercise is to become more responsible in different ways, some of which can be difficult for you. For example

- Don't answer back.
- Say *please* and *thank you*.
- Be kind to your friends.
- Clear the table.
- Clean your shoes.

Write each challenge in the notebook and write the date. Under the date, draw seven boxes, one for each day of the coming week. Then, every day, before going to bed, think about how well you met the challenge. If you think you did well, put an "X" in the box that corresponds to that day. If you think you did not meet the challenge that day, leave the box blank. At the end of the week, if there are blank boxes, carry on with the challenge for another week until you have filled all the boxes with an "X." Then, write "I am a responsible person" at the bottom of the page.

Follow the responsible leader

GAME

1. Choose a player who will lead the group.
2. Form a line, with the leader in front.
3. Follow the leader's instructions: if he runs, everybody runs.
4. The leader jumps, crawls, whistles, or hops—and the players have to follow him.
5. The leader's challenge is to be responsible in what he asks the players to do—making sure he does not ask them to do anything dangerous or too difficult.

*This week . . .
I will try to
be more
responsible
by . . .*

WEEK

44 Faith

• *Matthew 9:29*
Then touched he their eyes, saying, According to your faith be it unto you.

To have faith means to believe in something that cannot be seen or touched. Those blind men wanted their sight restored, and Jesus asked them if they believed he could cure them. They said they did, and Jesus cured them.

• **CHILDREN SOMETIMES SAY**
- How do we know God exists if we cannot see Him?

• **WHAT DO WE ANSWER?**
- Nobody has ever seen the wind, but we believe that it exists. Everybody notices the effects of the wind: the leaves on the trees move, the dust from the road swirls around, even roofs fly away when there is a high wind.

• **A FEW MINUTES TO THINK**
Nobody has ever seen God, but we can see all the good things He has done in nature, for example flowers, the sea, rivers, and stars.

Who knows what we will find!

EXPERIMENT

Material

A shoebox, objects with different textures (for example, a sponge, some cotton, a stone, some flour, and a potato), a piece of cloth, and glue.

1. On the front side of the shoebox, draw a rectangle and cut it out; it should be big enough to put your hand through.
2. Glue the cloth to the top part of the rectangle so it looks like a curtain.
3. Put one of the objects inside the box but don't let anybody see it.

Players will feel the object inside the box and guess what it is. The game continues with a change of objects.

Blind man's Bluff

GAME

Material
A scarf

One of the members of the group will use the scarf as a blindfold and will try to catch one of the players. He has to guess who it is. The player who has been tagged will be blindfolded next.

This week . . .
I will pray for the gift of more faith.

SEEING
What we can't see is harder to identify.

45 ACCEPTANCE

• *Genesis 4:6–7*
Why art thou wroth? and why is thy countenance fallen?
If thou doest well, shalt thou not be accepted?

These verses come from the story of Cain and Abel. Cain worked the land, and Abel was a sheep shepherd. Abel offered God the best he had, but Cain did not do the same.
God received favorably Abel's gift, but not Cain's, and Cain killed his brother out of envy.

• **CHILDREN SOMETIMES SAY**
- I want a mobile phone. I'm the only one in my class at school who doesn't have one!

• **WHAT DO WE ANSWER?**
- You should not get mad or envy what others have and you do not have—or need!

• **A FEW MINUTES TO THINK**
It is natural for children to envy others, whether it is because they want to have the same things their friends have or because something is the fashion. Sometimes, when they get what they want, they lose interest in it. They may feel that, if they don't get what they want, their parents don't love them, or their parents are too strict or other families are better than theirs. It is a question, then, of talking things through—even if they don't appear to accept what you are saying. If they learn not to envy what others have when they are young children, when they are older, they will be content with what they have.

People's envy
LET'S CHAT

Material

Wrapping paper or cardboard, adhesive tape, thick marker, and newspapers or television.

1. Look for situations in the world, at school, or in the family where envy exists.
2. Write them on a piece of wrapping paper or on the cardboard.
3. Discuss them.
- Was the conflict caused by envy, and has it brought about any good?
- Are there any solutions?

Look under the napkin
GAME—SURPRISE

Material

Bag with assorted sweets (for example, candies, chewing gum, and chocolates)

1. For a whole week, the children will find a sweet wrapped in their napkin or placed inside their glass at the meal table.
2. They are not allowed to swap their sweets—even if they don't like the sweet they get and they prefer the sweet somebody else has.
3. On the last day, everyone will get the same kind of sweet, and they can talk about what's happened during the week.

EXAMPLES
There is a lot of envy in the world, but there are also many good-hearted, loving people.

This week . . .
I will be content with what I have and with the little things I enjoy, and I will thank the Lord for them.

46 Serenity

• *Luke 4:28, 30*
And all they in the synagogue, when they heard these things, were filled with wrath. . . . But he passing through the midst of them went his way.

Jesus was in the synagogue reading a passage from the book of Isaiah that talked about helping the poor, freeing the captive, and so forth. Those who were listening to him did not like what he said. He didn't allow that to upset him; he just passed through their midst and went on his way.

• **CHILDREN SOMETIMES SAY**

- Somebody insulted me in the playground at school today, but I did not pay any attention. I walked away.

• **WHAT DO WE ANSWER?**

- Well done! It is much better to ignore these things. If you had reacted to them, they probably would have insulted you even more.

• **A FEW MINUTES TO THINK**

It is very difficult to remain calm in front of an injustice or when someone provokes you by insulting you. If you are aggressive, the consequences can be even worse.

Is it not better, after you've had a chance to think about it, to try to sort out the reason why the other person does not like you?

Little By little
SERENITY

Material
Wool in a tangle

Take some wool that has become tangled and patiently sort it out. Then one person holds the wool while the other winds it into a ball.

Don't lose your nerve!
LET'S CHAT

Think about some scenarios when you could lose your nerve, such as

- getting lost in the forest
- getting lost in a big city
- being robbed of your watch or mobile telephone
- getting bitten by a snake
- having a fire at home

Staying calm—keeping your serenity—will help you work out what to do.

This week . . .
I will try to stay calm and to be serene.

47 Service

• *1 Peter 4:10*
As every man hath received the gift, even so minister the same one to another, as good stewards of the manifold grace of God.

We all have gifts we can serve others with. We should be ready to use our gifts to help people in need—even if it means interrupting our favorite activities.

• CHILDREN SOMETIMES SAY
- I'm always the one you ask to set the table and pick up the toys! Why can't you ask someone else?

• WHAT DO WE ANSWER?
- Everybody has their own little jobs to do. I ask others to do what they can to help too.

• A FEW MINUTES TO THINK
Children don't always like to be asked to help—especially if it means they have to interrupt their favorite activity or TV program. We have to teach them to be willing to help. You might switch tasks, asking them to do different chores so they won't get bored always doing the same old thing. It helps, too, if you ask them to do something before they begin to watch TV or tell them that the chore can be done when their favorite program is over. Wise timing on your part sometimes helps foster cooperation on their part!

A joB for each Person

LET'S CHAT—PARTY

Find out the gifts each member of the group has, discuss them and decide how to put them to use. We all have gifts, and we should stress the importance of having these gifts and using them to serve others. Of course, it is not only a question of being willing to use the gifts, it is also necessary to know how to use them.

This week . . .
I will serve someone with my gifts by . . .

Let's organize a party

- The person with the gift of catering will prepare the sandwiches.
- The person with artistic gifts can draw.
- The person with nice handwriting will write the place cards so that everyone will know where to sit at the table.
- The person who can use the computer will type the menu.
- The person with musical gifts will play something or will choose the music for the party.
- The person who likes going shopping will be in charge of getting the ingredients for the sandwiches.

A recipe for ham and cheese rolled sandwiches

Ingredients for each sandwich: A slice of bread, two portions of soft cheese, a slice of cooked ham, and tin foil. (Other ingredients can be used if you want.)

1. Place some tin foil under the slice of bread.
2. With a knife, spread one portion of soft cheese over the bread.
3. Put the ham on top.
4. Spread the second portion of soft cheese over the ham.
5. Roll the slice of bread with the help of the tin foil.
6. Put the sandwich in the fridge for a few hours.

The sandwiches can be served wrapped in the tin foil with a ribbon around them to decorate them; but they can also be served without the tin foil, sliced and presented nicely on a plate.

WEEK

48 Thankfulness

• *Psalm 104:33*
I will sing unto the Lord as long as I live: I will sing praise to my God while I have my being.

This psalm is a song of thankfulness to our God, creator of the universe.

• **CHILDREN SOMETIMES SAY**
- I don't want this meal. I don't like it.

• **WHAT DO WE ANSWER?**
- It is good food. You should be thankful to have such good food to eat!

• **A FEW MINUTES TO THINK**
We can tell the children that we are lucky because we have food to eat several times a day; there are many people in the world who don't have that. We should also be thankful to the person who has prepared the food for us.

We give thanks with a song

SONG

We can sing this song before each meal.

"The more people we are at the table, at the table, at the table
The more people we are at the table, the happier we will be".

We say thank you for everything

GAME

Each person gives thanks for one thing on the table or for one of the ingredients.

For example:
"Thank you for the water" or "Thank you for the salt". The game continues until someone repeats a thank-you for something already mentioned, and that person loses the game.

This week . . .
I will remember to say thank you for . . .

WEEK 49 HAPPINESS

• *Ephesians 6:2–3*
Honour thy father and mother; (which is the first commandment with promise;)
That it may be well with thee, and thou mayest live long on the earth.

St. Paul reminds us, in his letter to the Ephesians, that those who honor their father and their mother will have a happy life.

● **CHILDREN SOMETIMES SAY**
- Why are you happy?

● **WHAT DO WE ANSWER?**
- I am happy because I love you and because I am loved by you. That is what makes me happy!

● **A FEW MINUTES TO THINK**
It is good to explore with children what true happiness is—what makes us happy. It is important for them to understand that happiness does not always come because of material possessions. Explore with the children what makes them happy.

The Prodigal son

THE STORY

There was a man who had two sons. One day, the younger son asked his father for the money that was his, and his father gave it to him. The son went far away and had great fun, and he spent all his money. He had to accept a job taking care of pigs. He felt lonely and sad, and he was hungry. He would have eaten the food the pigs were eating, but nobody offered him any.

Then one day, he remembered the way his father treated his servants, and he thought that he would go back and ask to be one of his father's servants. "I will return to my father's house and ask his forgiveness" he said to himself.

When the father saw his younger son in the distance, he rushed out to meet him. He embraced him and kissed him. He was so happy to have the son he had lost back again.

The younger son said to his father: "Forgive me and make me your servant."

But his father said, "Give him the best robe, put a ring on his finger, and sandals on his feet. Prepare a celebration, for my son has come back home."

The older son was very angry. His father told him: "My son, everything I have is yours, but we must be happy because I have found the son I had lost." (You can read the story in Luke 15:11–31.)

This week . . .
I will notice the things that make me happy!

Advent Calendar

HANDICRAFT

Advent is a time of anticipation and happiness when we anxiously wait for Christmas.

Material
24 pieces of cardboard 4 x 12 in, tracing paper, glue, pencil, markers, scissors, 24 pegs, stocking patterns from page 122.

For the stockings
1. Fold the 24 pieces of cardboard in half along the longer side.
2. Use the pattern to cut out the stockings, and glue the two pieces together along the edges, except at the top.
3. Paint the stockings.
4. When they are dry, put a small surprise inside each one and hang them out on the line.
5. Take some pegs and write a number on each one, from 1 to 24.
6. From December 1st to December 24th, invite someone at home or in the classroom to take out the surprise of the day.

50 courage

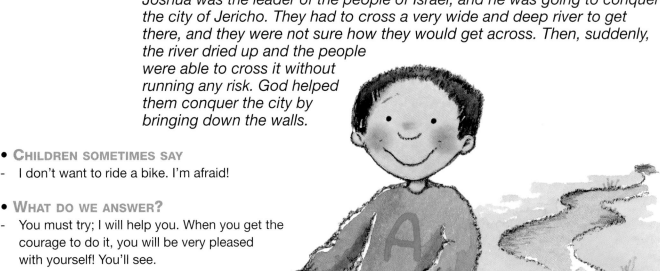

- *Joshua 1:9*
Have not I commanded thee? Be strong and of a good courage; be not afraid, neither be thou dismayed: for the Lord thy God is with thee whithersoever thou goest.

Joshua was the leader of the people of Israel, and he was going to conquer the city of Jericho. They had to cross a very wide and deep river to get there, and they were not sure how they would get across. Then, suddenly, the river dried up and the people were able to cross it without running any risk. God helped them conquer the city by bringing down the walls.

- **CHILDREN SOMETIMES SAY**
- I don't want to ride a bike. I'm afraid!

- **WHAT DO WE ANSWER?**
- You must try; I will help you. When you get the courage to do it, you will be very pleased with yourself! You'll see.

- **A FEW MINUTES TO THINK**
Children sometimes express their fear when they have to learn something new or make a decision or go to an unknown place. It is up to us to make them feel safe and confident so they can act with courage.

A fortress
HANDICRAFT—GAME

Material
Clay or modeling clay, string, a square piece of wood, plastic or cardboard, tools to model the clay, some very small boxes, wooden popsicle sticks, paint and brushes, straw or dry grass, scissors, glue, and a thick permanent marker.

The walls
1. Using the string, cut a few blocks of clay and model 4 or 5 watchtowers.
2. Model rectangular pieces to go from tower to tower.
3. Assemble the pieces on the square base.

The gate
1. Use two wooden sticks for the sides, and place other sticks between them.
2. Stand the gate in clay.
3. Paint the gate.

The town
1. Build and paint the boxes.
2. With the marker, draw and paint doors, windows, cracks on the walls, and any other decoration.
3. Cut pieces of straw and glue them to the top of each box for roofs.

Now you can finish assembling the fortress, and you can play with it or look at it and think about what it must have been like to live in such a place.

This week . . .
I will try to have the courage to do something I have been afraid to do until now.

51 UPrightness

• *1 Timothy 2:2*
For kings, and for all that are in authority; that we may lead a quiet and peaceable life in all godliness and honesty.

An upright person should first of all be a grateful person, peaceful and loving—someone whom others trust and respect.

• **CHILDREN SOMETIMES SAY**
- I found this wallet in the park. There is money in it. Now I'll be able to buy that toy I saw in the window at the toy shop.

• **WHAT DO WE ANSWER?**
- We can't keep this wallet. It doesn't belong to us, and the person who lost it must be really worried. We have to hand it over to the police.

• **A FEW MINUTES TO THINK**
Every day, we face temptations and have to think about which is the right or wrong thing to do. Finding a wallet in the park is one example.

Help the children to understand the importance of being honest by asking them what they would do if they found any of the following:
• a coin
• a baby's shoe
• a handbag
• a watch

Zaccheus

THE STORY

Zaccheus was a very rich man. He was a tax collector and had no friends because he always overcharged people when he collected their taxes, and nobody liked him.

Jesus went to visit the town where Zaccheus lived, and Zaccheus wanted to see him, but there was a big crowd. Everybody was taller than him, and he could not see anything.

He decided to climb a tree so he could see Jesus when he went by.

When Jesus was passing the tree, he looked up and said, "Zaccheus, come down right away. Today I must go to your house." Zaccheus was very happy because Jesus wanted to be his friend, and he said, "Lord, I will give half my money to the poor and will return to everybody fourfold the money I cheated out of them."

From that day on, Zaccheus was fair and respectable and stopped cheating people.

We Perform a Play

DRAMATIZATION

Act out Zaccheus's story.

This week . . .
I will remember to be upright—especially if I find something that doesn't belong to me!

FRIENDS
To have good friends means that you are loved because you are trusted.

52 HOSPITALITY

• *Matthew 25:35*
For I was an hungred, and ye gave me meat: I was thirsty, and ye gave me drink: I was a stranger, and ye took me in.

When people arrive in a foreign country, the first thing they want is to feel welcome and to find a job they feel comfortable with.

• CHILDREN SOMETIMES SAY

- A new girl came to our class today, but we didn't think she was very nice; she doesn't speak a word of English!

• WHAT DO WE ANSWER?

- You can't judge her just because she doesn't speak English. She doesn't know any of you and probably misses her friends from home. Give her a chance and make her feel welcome.

• A FEW MINUTES TO THINK

Talk about how a foreigner should be made to feel welcome. Talk about the difficulties they face when they arrive in a new place. Christmas is a time when it is especially important to invite anyone who is lonely into our homes.

Poem in a frame

HANDICRAFT

Listen to this poem:

*A friend always comes too late
and goes too soon.
Visitor, who are you?
If you are a friend, I welcome you
with all my heart!
If you are a foreigner, hospitality awaits you.
If you are an enemy, kindness will keep you here.*

Material
Cardboard, markers, glue, ribbons, wool, strips of colored plastic, ruler, scissors, cutter, hole puncher.

1. Write the poem on a piece of cardboard.
2. On another piece of cardboard the same size, cut out a rectangle in the center.
3. Glue that piece of cardboard to the big piece so that the poem will appear in the center of the rectangle.
4. With a hole puncher, make a few holes all round the cardboard.
5. Weave colored ribbons or string in and out of the holes.

The result will be an attractive frame you can hang on the wall by the front door of your house to welcome visitors.

Christmas candlesticks
HANDICRAFT

Material
Glass jars, small candles, paint, permanent markers, brush.

Process
1. Paint the outside of the jar with Christmas decorations (for example, stars, bells, or the face of a smiling Santa Claus).
2. Place the candle inside.

You can have one candlestick per person or just a few all together in the middle of the table. Light them when you sit down at table.

This week . . .
I will be especially welcoming to any visitor I meet.

Patterns

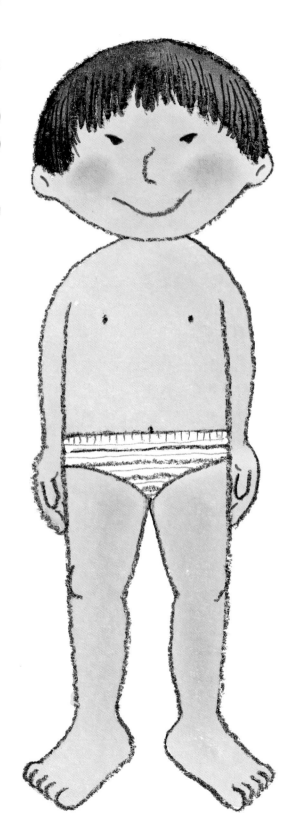

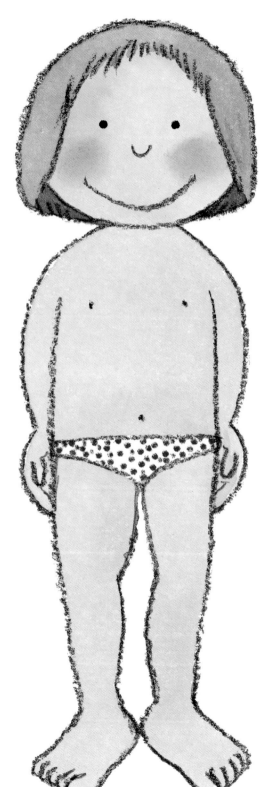

Let's cut out paper clothes – page 11

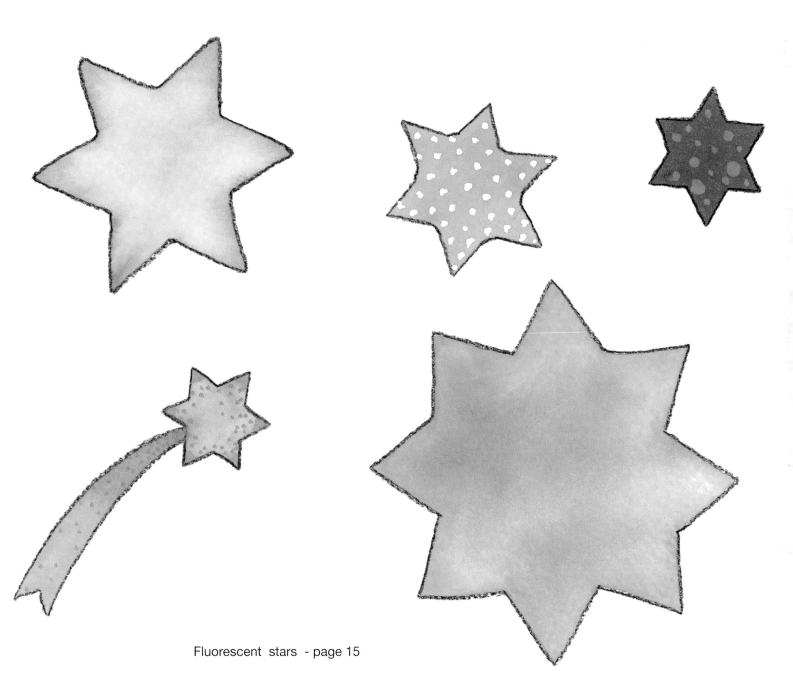

Fluorescent stars - page 15

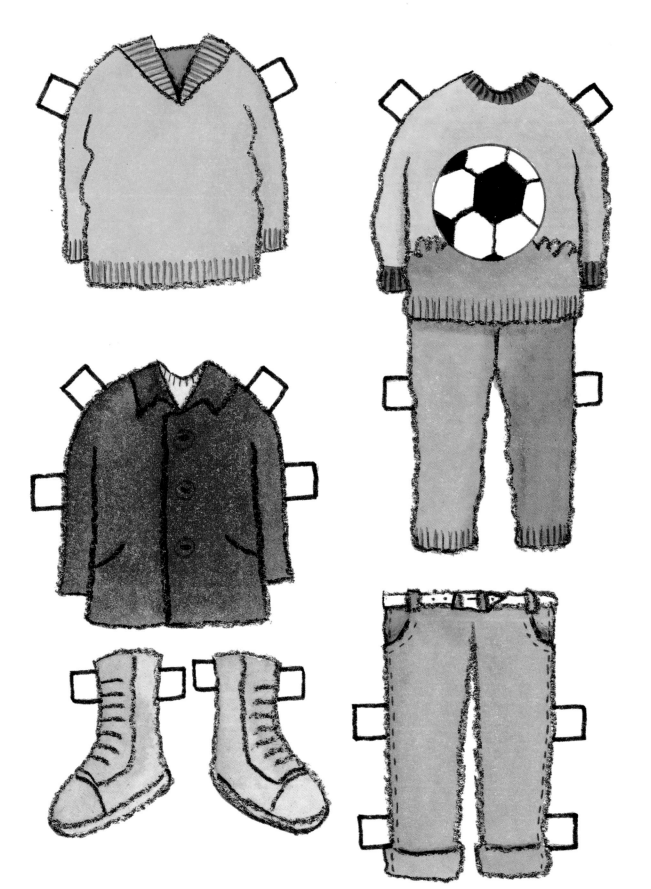

Let's cut out paper clothes – page 11

Let's cut out paper clothes – page 11

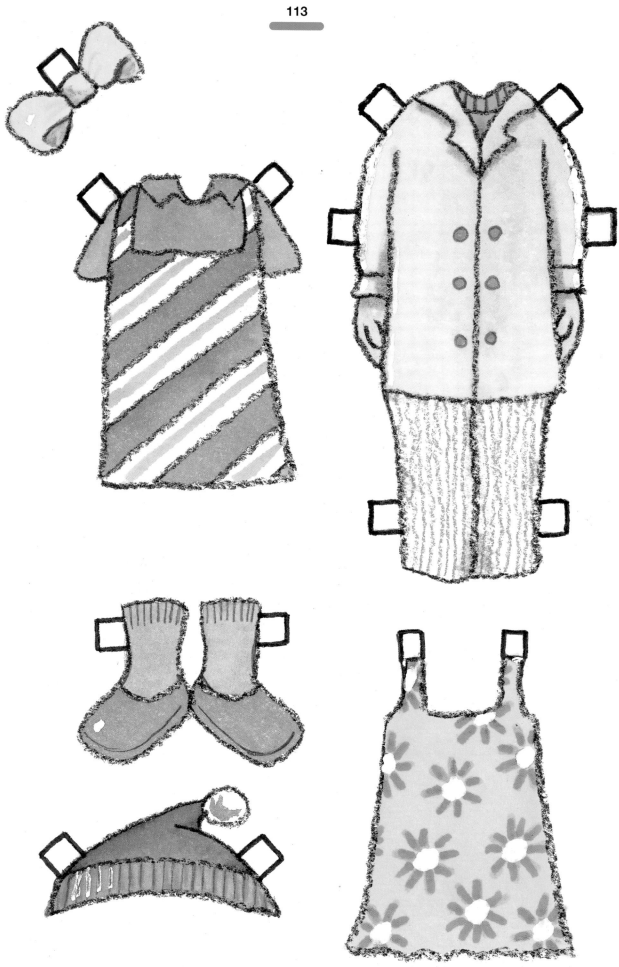

Mask-making - page 51

Let's make a puppet theater - page 55

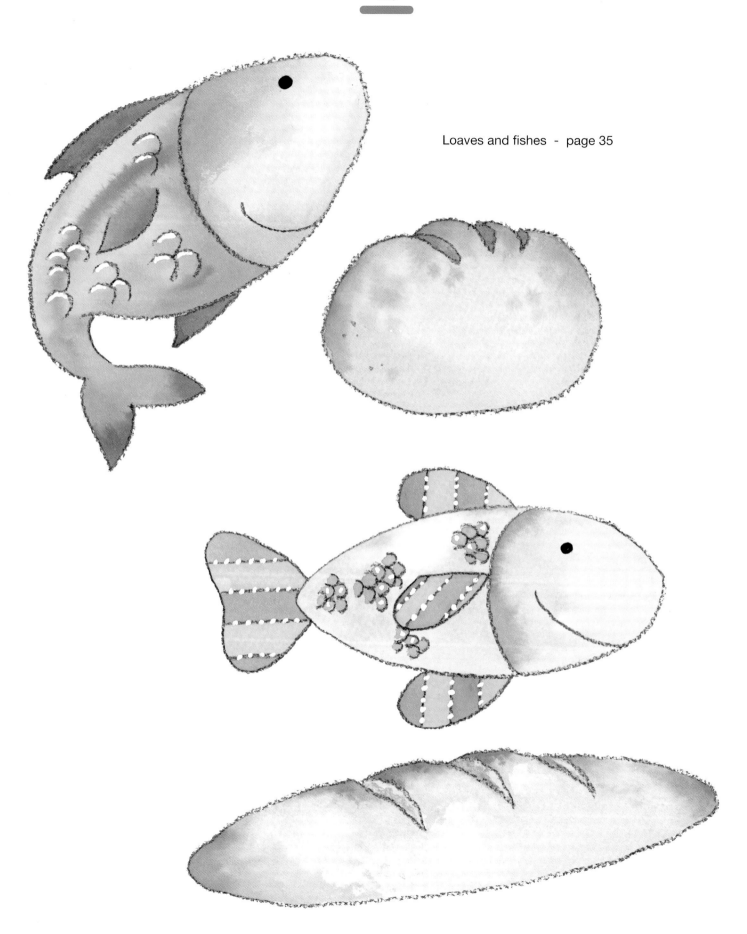

Loaves and fishes - page 35

Let's go fishing - page 69

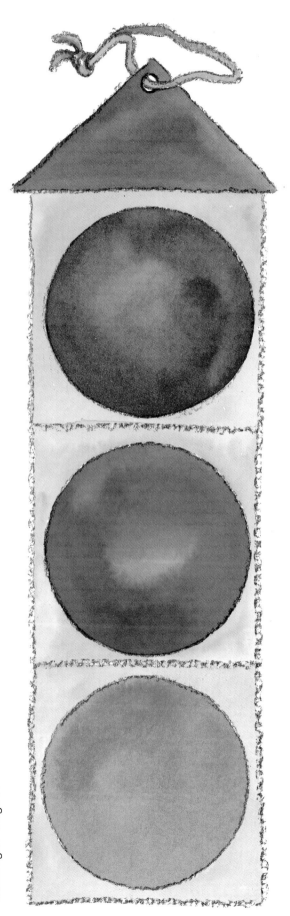

Traffic light - Page 77

Advent calendar - page 101

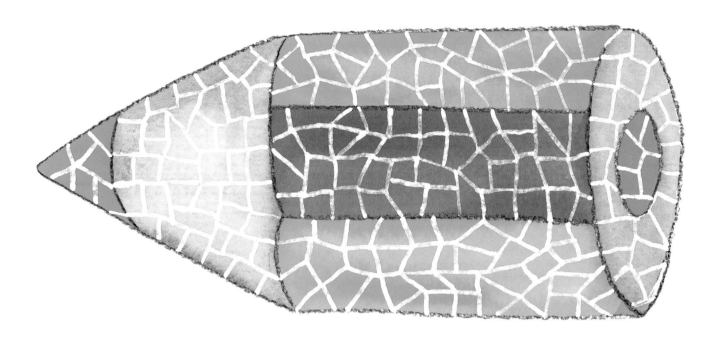

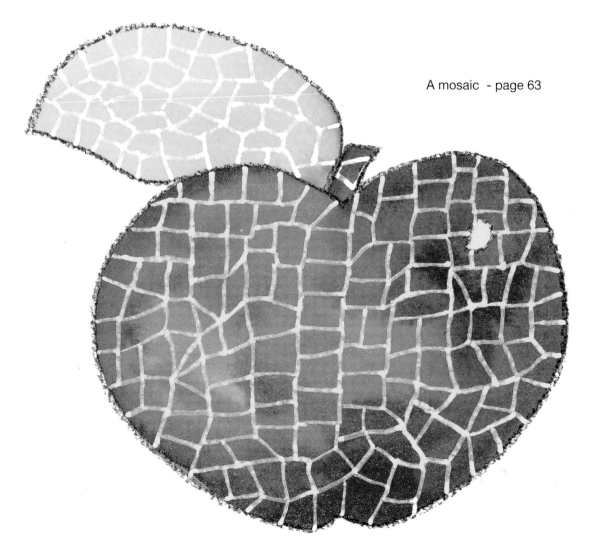

A mosaic - page 63

Biblical texts and reflections

ACCEPTANCE → Genesis 4:6–7
Why art thou wroth? and why is thy countenance fallen? If thou doest well, shalt thou not be accepted?

These verses come from the story of Cain and Abel. Cain worked the land, and Abel was a sheep shepherd. Abel offered God the best he had, but Cain did not do the same.

God received favorably Abel's gift, but not Cain's, and Cain killed his brother out of envy.

AVAILABILITY → 1 Thessalonians 5:15
See that none render evil for evil unto any man; but ever follow that which is good, both among yourselves, and to all men.

When we decide to do something for someone, we should do it happily so that the person being helped will see that we want to be there for them. It is important to be available to others—even when that sometimes means that we have to stop doing something we like doing.

BEAUTY → Psalm 8: 3–4
When I consider thy heavens, the work of thy fingers, the moon and the stars, which thou hast ordained;

What is man, that thou art mindful of him? and the son of man, that thou visitest him?

Think about the world around us. Notice the beauty of the trees and the flowers, of all the different people and animals. Look up at the sky and the clouds: the sun in the daytime and the moon and stars at night.

CHEERFULNESS → Psalm 30:11
Thou hast turned for me my mourning into dancing: thou hast put off my sackcloth, and girded me with gladness.

David was very sad, and he asked God for help; God cheered him up.

COMMITMENT → Deuteronomy 26:17
Thou hast avouched the Lord this day to be thy God, and to walk in his ways, and to keep his statutes, and his commandments, and his judgments, and to hearken unto his voice.

Once we have decided to love the Lord and do as he tells us, you will see that he will always take care of us.

COMMUNICATION → 1 Samuel 3:10
And the Lord came, and stood, and called as at other times, Samuel, Samuel. Then Samuel answered, Speak; for thy servant heareth.

Samuel was a boy who paid attention to God talking to him; he listened to God.

CONFIDENCE → Psalm 70:1
Make haste, O God, to deliver me; make haste to help me, O Lord.

Many times, when we feel lost or in difficulty, we ask help from someone we know will lend us a hand. In this psalm, David asks the Lord to help him be confident.

CONSISTENCY → Matthew 7:12
Therefore all things whatsoever ye would that men should do to you, do ye even so to them: for this is the law and the prophets.

Jesus tells us: love others as you love yourself. It is a fundamental principle of our behavior.

COURAGE → Joshua 1:9
Have not I commanded thee? Be strong and of a good courage; be not afraid, neither be thou dismayed: for the Lord thy God is with thee whithersoever thou goest.

Joshua was the leader of the people of Israel, and he was going to conquer the city of Jericho. They had to cross a very wide and deep river to get there, and they were not sure how they would get across. Then, suddenly, the river dried up and the people were able to cross it without running any risk. God helped them conquer the city by bringing down the walls.

DILIGENCE → Ecclesiastes 5:12
The sleep of a labouring man is sweet, whether he eat little or much: but the abundance of the rich will not suffer him to sleep.

A good worker is a person who enjoys doing his job and feels satisfied when it is finished.

DISCERNMENT → Luke 20:25
And he said unto them, Render therefore unto Cæsar the things which be Cæsar's, and unto God the things which be God's.

At the time of the Roman empire, the political authorities spread the rumor that Jesus was telling people not to pay tributes to Caesar, who was the emperor. When the pharisees, who were a religious group, asked Jesus what they should do, Jesus said, "you should not confuse what belongs to God with what belongs to the empire."

DISCRETION → Matthew 9:30
And their eyes were opened; and Jesus straitly charged them, saying, See that no man know it.

When Jesus helped someone, he did not brag about it. As his followers, we should try to copy him in our behavior.

ENVIRONMENT → Genesis 1:28
And God blessed them, and God said unto them . . . have dominion over the fish of the sea, and over the fowl of the air, and over every living thing that moveth upon the earth.

This value is about knowing, loving, respecting, and defending our planet.

FAITH → Matthew 9:29
Then touched he their eyes, saying, According to your faith be it unto you.

To have faith means to believe in something that cannot be seen or touched. Those blind men wanted their sight restored, and Jesus asked them if they believed he could cure them. They said they did, and Jesus cured them.

FORGIVENESS → Matthew 6:12
And forgive us our debts, as we forgive our debtors.

When we forgive, we should forget and not hold a grudge.

FREEDOM → Galatians 5:13
For, brethren, ye have been called unto liberty; only use not liberty for an occasion to the flesh, but by love serve one another.

The apostle Paul calls the Jewish people to be free—free to be responsible, free to be without envy, without jealousy or rivalry.

FRIENDSHIP → John 15:15
Henceforth I call you not servants; for the servant knoweth not what his lord doeth: but I have called you friends; for all things that I have heard of my Father I have made known unto you.

God wants to be your friend, give you good advice, and be close to you when you need him.

GENEROSITY → Proverbs 11:17
The merciful man doeth good to his own soul: but he that is cruel troubleth his own flesh.

The generous person is the one who thinks of others, the one who helps without expecting anything back, the one who can forgive without resentment. Generosity does not make distinctions; generosity opens our hearts and enriches us.

GENUINENESS → Luke 6:43
For a good tree bringeth not forth corrupt fruit; neither doth a corrupt tree bring forth good fruit.

If people are genuine, you will see it in the way they behave. Equally, if people are not genuine but jealous and selfish, you will see that too in the way they behave.

GOODNESS → Psalm 113:7
He raiseth up the poor out of the dust, and lifteth the needy out of the dunghill.

The psalmist tells us about a God who is good, compassionate and just, who helps those in need no matter what their faith, race, sex, or age is.

GRATITUDE → Philippians 1:3
I thank my God upon every remembrance of you.

When the apostle Paul wrote these words, he was in prison. Paul had always appreciated the people who helped him, and in this letter addressed to the Philippians, he expressed his deep gratitude to them because they had helped him every time he needed it.

HAPPINESS → Ephesians 6:2–3
Honour thy father and mother; (which is the first commandment with promise;)
That it may be well with thee, and thou mayest live long on the earth.

St. Paul reminds us, in his letter to the Ephesians, that those who honor their father and their mother will have a happy life.

HONESTY → Proverbs 16:8
Better is a little with righteousness than great revenues without right.

The proverb tells us to be honest and to earn things honestly.

HOPE → Ephesians 1:12
That we should be to the praise of his glory, who first trusted in Christ.

Everybody has hope in something; the people who believe in God hope to see God one day.

HOSPITALITY → Matthew 25:35
For I was an hungred, and ye gave me meat: I was thirsty, and ye gave me drink: I was a stranger, and ye took me in.

When people arrive in a foreign country, the first thing they want is to feel welcome and to find a job they feel comfortable with.

HUMILITY → Matthew 21:5
Tell ye the daughter of Sion, Behold, thy King cometh

unto thee, meek, and sitting upon an ass, and a colt the foal of an ass.

When Jesus entered Jerusalem, people welcomed him with palm branches.

This king is special. This king is the king of peace. This king came and lived among us. He had no special privileges.

INTEGRITY → Matthew 7:20
Wherefore by their fruits ye shall know them.

If we look at fruit trees in the early spring, we see only their leaves. We probably don't know whether they are pear trees, apple trees, or cherry trees. But if we see the same trees in the summertime, we will see the fruit growing on the trees, and we will see what kind of trees they are.

People are also recognized by their "fruits"—that is, by everything they do, whether good or bad.

JOY → Psalm 122:1
I was glad when they said unto me, Let us go into the house of the Lord.

It is good to go to church; it is a place where we meet people, share our faith, and think about what is happening in our lives.

JUSTICE → Proverbs 14:34
Righteousness exalteth a nation: but sin is a reproach to any people.

Solomon tells us that a just nation is one that allows all of its members to have the same opportunities. If we want to be proud of our people, we must work with justice.

LOVE → Acts 9:36
Now there was at Joppa a certain disciple named Tabitha, which by interpretation is called Dorcas: this woman was full of good works and almsdeeds which she did.

Dorcas had many friends. She made clothes for people in need, and she liked to help them. The whole town loved Dorcas because she loved her people.

LOYALTY → Ecclesiastes 5:4
When thou vowest a vow unto God, defer not to pay it; for he hath no pleasure in fools: pay that which thou hast vowed.

In olden times, the word "given" was very important. If two people gave their word about something, there was no need for documents because the word they had given was enough. This verse from Ecclesiastes tells us that if we are not sure of what we promise, it is better not to promise it at all because a promise should always be kept.

MERCY → Jonah 4:2
And he prayed unto the Lord, and said, I pray thee, O Lord, was not this my saying, when I was yet in my country? Therefore I fled before unto Tarshish: for I knew that thou art a gracious God, and merciful, slow to anger, and of great kindness, and repentest thee of the evil.

Jonah, after spending three days in the belly of a whale, asked God to save him, and he did. He wanted God to show him mercy as well.

OBEDIENCE → Genesis 6:22
Thus did Noah; according to all that God commanded him, so did he.

Noah was pleased to obey, and God rewarded him.

OPENNESS → Psalm 46:9
Come, behold the works of the Lord.

The psalmist invites us to know how great God is, to admire his works and be grateful for everything he has done for us all.

PATIENCE → Proverbs 15:18
A wrathful man stirreth up strife: but he that is slow to anger appeaseth strife.

It is better to be at peace than to be a worrier.

PEACE → Matthew 5:9
Blessed are the peacemakers: for they shall be called the children of God.

Working toward peace is working to achieve a society free of hatred, resentment, and injustice. The person who works for peace is happy because she is working for the happiness of other people.

PRUDENCE → Proverbs 2:11
Discretion shall preserve thee, understanding shall keep thee.

Prudence is a virtue. We should think about what we say and do before we say or do it. Prudence helps us act more sensibly.

REFLECTIVENESS → Proverbs 16:23
The heart of the wise teacheth his mouth, and addeth learning to his lips.

Reflectiveness is to take time to think something over. This is sometimes difficult because it requires time and space.

The writer of this proverb tells us that wise people take some time to think before they speak. They reflect on what they are going to say, and so they are more effective when they speak.

RELIABILITY → James 5:12
But above all things, my brethren, swear not, neither by heaven, neither by the earth, neither by any other oath: but let your yea be yea; and your nay, nay; lest ye fall into condemnation.

When someone asks us to do something, we should think carefully before saying "yes" or "no," and we should mean what we say!

RESPONSIBILITY → Deuteronomy 31:8
And the Lord, he it is that doth go before thee; he will be with thee, he will not fail thee, neither forsake thee.

When Moses grew old, he no longer was the guide for the people of Israel. The new guide would be Joshua. Moses told Joshua not to fear because the Lord would be with him and would not leave him.

RESPECT → 1 Peter 3:15
But sanctify the Lord God in your hearts: and be ready always to give an answer to every man that asketh you a reason of the hope that is in you with meekness and fear.

In ancient Greece, people were considered to be intelligent when they were able to defend their ideas respectfully, having pondered them in a reflective way.

SELF-DISCIPLINE → Proverbs 4:13
Take fast hold of instruction; let her not go: keep her; for she is thy life.

We all have to learn new things; we never stop learning!

SERENITY → Luke 4:28, 30
And all they in the synagogue, when they heard these things, were filled with wrath. . . . But he passing through the midst of them went his way.

Jesus was in the synagogue reading a passage from the book of Isaiah that talked about helping the poor, freeing the captive, and so forth. Those who were listening to him did not like what he said. He didn't allow that to upset him; he just passed through their midst and went on his way.

SERVICE → 1 Peter 4:10
As every man hath received the gift, even so minister the same one to another, as good stewards of the manifold grace of God.

We all have gifts we can serve others with. We should be ready to use our gifts to help people in need—even if it means interrupting our favorite activities.

SIMPLICITY → Acts 2:46
And they, continuing daily with one accord in the temple, and breaking bread from house to house, did eat their meat with gladness and singleness of heart.

The first Christians lived in a community. They went to the temple every day. They shared what they had without making a big fuss.

SINCERITY → Proverbs 11:20
They that are of a froward heart are abomination to the Lord: but such as are upright in their way are his delight.

God wants us to be honest, sincere, spontaneous, and frank.

SOLIDARITY → Acts 4:32
And the multitude of them that believed were of one heart and of one soul: neither said any of them that ought of the things which he possessed was his own; but they had all things common.

The first Christians lived together, and everything they had was for the benefit of all. Many of them, like Barnabas (who owned a field) sold their possessions and gave all their money to the community.

THANKFULNESS → Psalm 104:33
We all have gifts we can serve others with. We should be ready to use our gifts to help people in need—even if it means interrupting our favorite activities.

This psalm is a song of thankfulness to our God, creator of the universe.

TRUST → Proverbs 3:5
Trust in the Lord with all thine heart; and lean not unto thine own understanding.

To trust is to have faith that God takes care of us and guides our lives.

UPRIGHTNESS → 1 Timothy 2:2
For kings, and for all that are in authority; that we may lead a quiet and peaceable life in all godliness and honesty.

An upright person should first of all be a grateful person, peaceful and loving—someone whom others trust and respect.

UNSELFISHNESS → John 6:9
There is a lad here, which hath five barley loaves, and two small fishes: but what are they among so many?

Jesus's disciples had to feed about five thousand people, and they didn't know how to do it. Nearby there was a young boy who had five loaves of bread and two fishes. He was willing to share what he had, and he gave it all to Jesus, who multiplied it—making it enough for everyone.

WISDOM → Proverbs 8:10
Receive my instruction, and not silver; and knowledge rather than choice gold.

People young and old—even small children—want to know how to make the right choices in life.

Sayville Library
88 Greene Avenue
Sayville, NY 11782

MAR 2 8 2012

Original title: *Actividades en Familia*

Original texts: Laura Blanco and Silvia Carbonell

Illustrations: Rosa Maria Curto

Editorial director: Ona Pons

Graphics: Gemser Publications, S.L.

© Gemser Publications, S.L. 2002

08329 Teia (Barcelona) – Espana

English Edition

Scripture texts: from the King James Version of the Bible

Project director: Rina Risitano, fsp

English translation editor: Diana Klein, BA, MA
Catechetical Adviser in Westminster Diocese, England

Cover design © 2011 by Lyle Mortimer

Published by Bonneville Books, an imprint of Cedar Fort, Inc.,

2373 W. 700 S., Springville, UT 84663

Distributed by Cedar Fort, Inc., www.cedarfort.com

ISBN 978-1-59955-861-5

Printed in China

All rights reserved.
No part of this publication may be reproduced
in any form or by any means, including: printing,
electronic, mechanical, photocopying, recording or
otherwise, without the prior written permission
of the rights' owner.